THE   BOOK   OF

COOKIES

T H E · B O O K · O F

COOKIES

PAT ALBUREY

Photography by
JON STEWART
assisted by Alister Thorpe

HPBooks

ANOTHER BEST SELLING VOLUME FROM HPBooks

Published by HPBooks, a division of Price Stern Sloan, Inc.
360 North La Cienega Boulevard, Los Angeles, California 90048
1st Printing

Home Economist: Pat Alburey
Color separation by J. Film Process Ltd, Bangkok, Thailand
Printed by New Interlitho S.p.A., Milan

By arrangement with Salamander Books Ltd. and Merehurst Press, London.
© Copyright Merehurst Limited 1988

Library of Congress Cataloging-in-Publication Data
Alburey, Pat.
  The book of cookies.

  Includes index.
  1. Cookies.   I. Title.
TX772.A37   1987   641.8'654   87-21244

CONTENTS

AUTHOR

Pat Alburey is a home economist with a special interest in baking and desserts. Her background includes experience in food photography, recipe development and teaching.

THE BOOK OF COOKIES

INTRODUCTION

Cookie is the name given to an infinite number of small plain, sweet or semisweet confections that have, over the years, become great favorites the world over with adults and children alike. Savory cookies are equally as popular, and are often called crackers. In fact, the earliest cookies were not sweet: they were simply hard flat rounds of unleavened flour and water paste.

From their humble beginnings, cookies have developed through the centuries into the irresistible delicacies we know them to be today. Along the way famous classics have evolved such as gingerbread, florentines, brandy snaps and shortbread. This book contains recipes for them all, plus many others ranging from simple oatcakes to a magnificent gingerbread house. There are over 100 recipes, with something to suit all tastes: homey, chunky cookies; plain and rich ones; those that are crisp, light and delicate; savory and good-for-you cookies; and special ones for the festive times of the year. There are even some recipes that do not have to be baked at all.

Most cookies have a crisp texture, be it the brittle crispness of brandy snaps or the harder crunchier crispness like that of gingersnaps. However, some cookies are much softer in texture and almost cake-like, such as brownies and those with a soft topping.

You do not have to be an experienced cook to be able to make cookies. They are exceptionally easy to make, requiring surprisingly little or no special equipment for making them. Most are so simple that children can make them. You will be surprised at just how many different types of cookies can be made from relatively few ingredients.

Cookies can be served from breakfast to bedtime. Make a lively start to the day by serving warm oatcakes with butter and jam, or with something savory like cheese, if you prefer. A coffee break is a good time to indulge in a few cookies as they are exceptionally good with coffee, and help to fill the gap until lunchtime. Finding a few wrapped cookies in a brown bag lunch is a special treat for anyone. Formal afternoon tea can be graced with an elegant selection of dainty cookies. Enhance creamy desserts, sorbets and ice creams by serving them with thin, crisp, wafer-like cookies, such as Langues de Chat. Begin a dinner party with style by serving homemade savory Blue-Cheese Nibbles, Pretzels and Sesame Sticks with before-dinner drinks and your guests will certainly get the conversation going. End the dinner with coffee and a selection of sinfully tempting cookies from the no-bake recipes or with almond cookies such as Almond Flowers or Amaretti. One or two cookies with a hot drink at bedtime will help you to relax after a busy day.

The aroma of freshly baked cookies is as enjoyable as the pleasure of making and eating them. If you have not already discovered the pleasures of cookie making, beware, this book can become addictive—happy cookie making!

EQUIPMENT

The delightful thing about cookie making is that it requires a minimum of essential equipment. Measuring cups, measuring spoons, a mixing bowl, rolling pin, spatula, baking sheet and cooling rack are the few things you will need to make a vast number of different cookies. If you would like to widen your repertoire, however, you may want to consider investing in some extra equipment. Read the following first to help you make wise choices.

Equipment for Preparing Cookie Doughs
In all baking accurate measuring is important. Standard measuring cups and spoons for dry ingredients are essential. For liquid measurements you will need an accurate liquid measuring cup. A large sifter is necessary for the even blending of flour with leavening agents and spices.

Equipment for Rolling Out
The rolling pin should be fairly long with smooth rounded ends; fancy handles and knobbed ends will mark the dough. However, there are ridged rolling pins made especially for the purpose of marking a rolled-out dough attractively, with simple straight lines or crisscross patterns.

Any smooth work surface or a large wooden pastry board can be used for rolling out cookie doughs. Although it is not essential, a large marble slab is an asset, particularly for the richer, softer doughs.

Equipment for Shaping
Simple shapes can be cut by hand with a thin-bladed knife. A pastry wheel will give a decorative edge to simple shapes.

Cutters can be bought in all shapes and sizes. When buying shaped cutters, make sure they have a good cutting edge which will cut through the dough cleanly and give a well-defined outline. Metal cutters are usually best; unfortunately, plastic ones do not always cut well. All cookie cutter measurements in this book were taken across the cutting edge.

For quick cutting out, a rolling cookie cutter is very useful. All you have to do is roll it across the rolled-out dough.

Many doughs and meringues are formed with a piping bag and tip. Choose a bag with a welded seam as opposed to a stitched seam so that the mixture will not ooze out. Metal piping tips give a more defined shape than plastic ones.

A mechanical cookie press is a must for the enthusiast. They come complete with an assortment of discs to produce very professional-looking, fancy shapes, and enable a vast number of cookies to be made quickly.

A luxury item is a shortbread mold. They are fairly expensive and are really only worth buying if you make a lot of shortbread.

For no-bake and bar cookies, a shallow cake pan is essential. Beware of some of the thinner metal pans that buckle from the oven's heat.

Equipment for Baking and Cooling

Baking sheets also should be made of heavy metal to prevent buckling. Buy the largest size your oven will hold so you can bake many cookies at once.

Nonstick parchment paper or waxed paper is the perfect answer to preventing rich doughs from sticking to baking sheets.

A flexible spatula is useful for removing cookies from baking sheets. One or two wire racks are essential for cooling cookies.

Equipment for Finishing

The majority of cookies are finished by simply sprinkling powdered or granulated sugar over them. A small fine sifter is ideal for this purpose.

A pastry brush is perfect for brushing cookies with glazes.

Care of Equipment

Metal baking sheets and metal cookie cutters will become rusty if they are not dried well after washing. Place them in a warm oven to dry before storing.

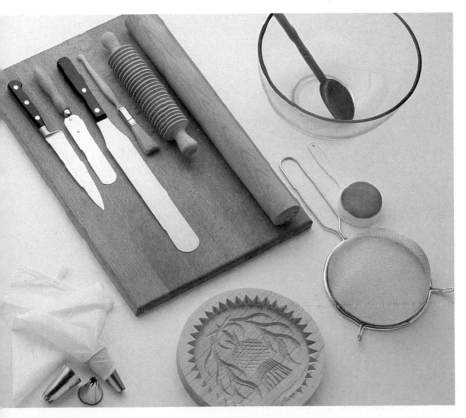

METHODS

While cookie making may appear to be a very complex affair, it really isn't at all. Although cookies can be made in an infinite variety of shapes, sizes, textures and flavors, the basic methods for making them are relatively few, and quite simple. They are the traditional cut-in, creamed, whisked, and melting methods; plus a few abstract ones for cookies that do not have to be baked, and for those that are made from meringue.

Cutting-In Method

Used to make very plain to very rich cookies. The dough is usually rolled out, then cut in shapes. It is sometimes rolled into shapes by hand.

Butter is incorporated into the flour by being cut in with a pastry blender until the mixture resembles fine bread crumbs. To prevent the dough from becoming soft and sticky, particularly when using a very high proportion of butter to flour, use cold firm butter. Handle the dough lightly and as little as possible. The texture of the finished cookie will vary according to the proportion of butter and sugar to flour. The higher the butter content, the softer the cookie. The lower the butter content and the higher the sugar content, the crisper the cookie. After the butter has been cut into the flour, the mixture is bound together with whole egg, egg yolks or milk to form a dough firm enough to roll out. Large eggs were used throughout this book, unless otherwise stated in the recipe. When a high proportion of butter is used, as for some short-breads, no binding ingredient is required.

Creamed Method

Produces a varying range of textures, from the crisp and brittle, to the soft and melt-in-the-mouth variety. The dough can be made firm enough to be rolled out with a rolling pin or rolled into shape by hand; soft enough to be squeezed through a piping tip or cookie press; or very soft, to be dropped from a spoon onto a baking sheet.

Softened butter is beaten with sugar until it is very creamy in appearance, light and fluffy in texture. Either a hand-held electric mixer or a wooden spoon can be used for creaming. During the beating, air is trapped within the mixture, which when baked causes the dough to rise making a light crisp cookie. Because much of this air is knocked out during the kneading and rolling-out process, a little additional leavening agent (such as baking powder) is added to some doughs.

Creamed doughs will be softer than those made by the cutting-in method. Most can be kneaded and rolled out immediately, but some need to be chilled to make them firm enough to roll out. When this is absolutely necessary, refrigeration is recommended in the recipe. If it is not specifically mentioned, and you do not feel confident enough to handle a softer dough, simply wrap the dough in plastic wrap and refrigerate it for a short time until firm. Do not allow the dough to become too hard as this will make it difficult to roll out and cause it to crack. Always refrigerate a dough rather than be tempted to knead in extra flour; the latter would change the texture of the cookie.

Whisked Method

Produces sponge-like cookies as well as those that are crisp and wafer thin. The mixture is spooned or piped onto baking sheets. Before the flour is added, eggs and sugar are beaten together until they are very thick and the mixture can retain its shape for five seconds after a spoon is drawn through the mixture. The beating can be done by hand, with a rotary beater or with a hand-held electric mixer.

Melting Method

This method can be used to produce anything from crisp melt-in-the mouth Florentines to harder crunchier cookies such as Gingersnaps and Gingerbread Men. Softer mixtures can be spooned onto baking sheets, firmer ones can be rolled into balls or be rolled out with a rolling pin. This type of dough has a high sugar content in the form of honey, molasses or corn syrup as well as sugar. The dough can be quite sticky when it is warm, but as it cools it becomes firmer and less sticky; so don't be tempted to knead in extra flour.

No-Bake Cookies

These are not really true cookies, but a delicious combination of ingredients which become firm and crisp when chilled. Although simple and quick to make, they do need long refrigeration for the ingredients to become firm. Many are bound together with chocolate. When melting chocolate, take great care not to overheat it. In some recipes the chocolate is melted in a saucepan over direct heat when it is combined with other ingredients, such as butter and water. In most cases, however, it is melted in a bowl over a pan of hot water. The bowl should be large enough to fit in the top of the pan exactly so that water cannot splash up into the chocolate. If water does get into the chocolate this will change its texture to thick and grainy. The bottom of the bowl should not be allowed to touch the water, and the water should be kept at a gentle simmer. Never allow the water to boil.

Meringue Cookies

These include Amaretti as well as many other dainty cookies perfect for serving with afternoon tea. Although some of the recipes call for the mixture to be piped, you can spoon the mixture into shape instead.

Refrigerator Cookies

So called because it is necessary to thoroughly chill the shaped dough before cutting it in slices for baking, and because the dough can be kept in the refrigerator for up to a week before it is baked.

Refrigerator cookie doughs are made by the traditional creaming method, and have a high butter and sugar content. The dough is quite soft to handle when it is first made, but after being shaped into rolls and refrigerated it becomes firm enough to be cut in thin slices for baking. These cookies spread as they are baked and should be well spaced on the baking sheets.

TECHNIQUES

Measuring Ingredients

For perfect results, it is absolutely necessary to measure ingredients accurately. Teaspoon measurements throughout this book are all level; dry ingredients should be leveled off with a small knife. Fluid measurements should all be read at eye level.

Preparing Baking Sheets

Every recipe gives definite instructions for the preparation of baking sheets. These instructions should be followed exactly. You may feel that using butter to grease a baking sheet is rather extravagant. However, cookies have very delicate flavors which can be very easily spoiled by using a strong-flavored margarine or shortening. You can, of course, use margarine or shortening when lining baking sheets with parchment or waxed paper. Why grease the sheet before lining? This is important to hold the paper in position, especially if you have a fan oven in which the fan tends to blow the paper up off the tray.

Rolling Out

When rolling out cookie doughs, you will need to flour both the work surface and the rolling pin to prevent the dough from sticking. Use only the smallest amount of flour necessary to prevent the dough from sticking. If you use too much the dough will become too dry and discolored. Move the dough frequently and flour underneath as you roll it out. Use only the lightest pressure needed to expand the dough. Too much flour on the surface of the dough will spoil the finished appearance of the cookies. Brush excess flour off with a small soft pastry brush before cutting out shapes.

Cutting Out

Dip cookie cutters in flour to prevent the dough from sticking to them. Pressing firmly, cut cleanly through the dough; do not twist the cookie cutter as this will spoil the shape. Remove shapes from the work surface to prepared baking sheets with a flexible spatula. Do not be tempted to pick them up with your fingers—they can easily be misshapen.

Baking

All baking times are given as a guide. As most ovens vary in temperature, the baking times necessary in your oven may differ a little either way. The type of baking sheet used can also affect the cooking time; some conduct heat better than others and can therefore speed up the baking time. When removed from the oven, most cookies are soft and should be left on the baking sheet for a few minutes before they are removed to wire racks to cool completely. Cookies become crisp as they cool. Some cookies, such as Brandy Snaps and Cigarettes Russes, have to be removed quickly from the baking sheet so that they can be shaped while they are hot. Explicit instructions are given in each recipe as to when and how the cookies should be removed from baking sheets.

Storing

With a few exceptions, most cookies should be stored in an airtight container to prevent them from absorbing moisture which makes them soften. A traditional cookie tin is the best storage container. Firmer cookies will keep longer than the softer ones. Never store cookies in the same container as cakes; the cookies will absorb moisture from the cakes and soften. When packing cookies for a lunch box or picnic, wrap them in foil or put them in a separate container to prevent them from absorbing flavors and moisture from other foods.

Presentation

As with all cooking, it is important to present homemade cookies well to make them extra-appealing. Serve them elegantly on china or glass plates, or on small cake stands—with or without a doily. They may be served in a more homey fashion in, or on, napkin-lined baskets.

Freezing

A good supply of cookie dough, already shaped or cut out if necessary, can be kept in the freezer ready to be baked when unexpected guests arrive, or as needed. First, freeze the unbaked cookies on foil-lined baking sheets until solid. Then remove from the baking sheets and pack in rigid containers for protection. By freezing the cookies first, they will remain separate when they are packed in the container, enabling you to remove just the number you require. Cover the container, label and return to the freezer. To bake, place frozen cookies on prepared baking sheets and bake as directed in the recipe, allowing a few extra minutes baking time.

—— CHOCOLATE-BRAN BARS ——

6 oz. semisweet chocolate, chopped
2 tablespoons butter
1 tablespoon molasses
2/3 cup (3 oz.) dried apricots, chopped
1/3 cup (2 oz.) pitted prunes, chopped
3 cups bran flake cereal

Grease a shallow 11'' x 7'' baking pan with butter; line bottom with parchment or waxed paper. Melt chocolate, butter and molasses together in a bowl placed over a pan of gently simmering water. Remove from heat.

Add apricots, prunes and cereal to chocolate mixture; mix thoroughly. Spread in prepared pan, smoothing top with the back of a spoon. Refrigerate 1 to 2 hours or until firmly set.

Loosen mixture from pan by running the tip of a knife around the inside edges of pan. Turn out onto a board and remove paper; turn mixture over. Cut in 24 pieces. Arrange bars neatly on a serving dish or store in an airtight container in a cool place for 2 to 3 days.

Makes 24 bars.

NUTTY BITES

1/4 cup unsalted butter
2 tablespoons light corn syrup
1/4 cup unsweetened cocoa
1/3 cup (2 oz.) raisins
2 cups cornflakes
1/2 cup hazelnuts, toasted, chopped

Put butter, corn syrup, cocoa and raisins in a medium-size saucepan; stir over gentle heat until butter melts and mixture is well blended. Remove from heat.

Stir the cornflakes and about 3/4 of the hazelnuts into the melted mixture. Spoon mixture into miniature paper baking cups placed on a baking sheet; sprinkle remaining hazelnuts over top. Refrigerate 1 hour or until set.

Arrange Nutty Bites attractively on a serving dish. If desired, use chopped candied cherries and toasted almonds instead of hazelnuts and raisins. Store in an airtight container in a cool place for 2 to 3 days.

Makes 30 to 40 cookies.

————EXOTIC TREATS————

2 cups (8 oz.) tropical fruit and nut mix
4 oz. semisweet chocolate pieces
1/4 cup unsalted butter
Zest of 2 large oranges

Grease a shallow 11'' x 7'' baking pan with butter; line bottom with parchment or waxed paper. Coarsely grind fruit and nut mix in a food processor or blender.

Melt chocolate and butter together in a small bowl placed over a pan of gently simmering water, stirring frequently. Mix in the processed nut mix and 1/2 of the orange zest. Spread mixture smoothly in prepared pan. Sprinkle remaining zest over top, pressing it in lightly. Refrigerate 1 to 2 hours or until firmly set.

Loosen set mixture from pan by carefully running the tip of a knife around the inside edges of the pan. Carefully turn out onto a board; remove paper. Turn mixture over and cut in 32 pieces. Store in an airtight container in a cool place for 2 to 3 days.

Makes 32 cookies.

— MUESLI & HONEY COOKIES —

2 tablespoons honey
1/4 cup unsalted butter
4 oz. semisweet chocolate, chopped
8 oz. muesli

Grease a shallow 11'' x 7'' baking pan with butter; line bottom with parchment or waxed paper. Place honey, butter and chocolate together in a large bowl placed over a pan of gently simmering water. Stir until butter melts; remove from heat.

Stir all but 1/4 cup of muesli into honey mixture. Spread in prepared pan, smoothing top with the back of a spoon. Sprinkle remaining muesli evenly on top, pressing gently into surface of mixture. Refrigerate 1 to 2 hours or until set.

Carefully remove muesli mixture from pan; remove paper. Cut in 8 squares. Cut each square in half to make 2 triangles. Arrange neatly on a serving dish or store in an airtight container in a cool place for 2 to 3 days.

Makes 16 cookies.

— CRÈME DE MENTHE COOKIES —

Base:
1/2 cup unsalted butter
1 tablespoon light corn syrup
12 oz. shortbread cookies, crushed

Frosting:
1/2 cup unsalted butter
1/2 cup whipping cream
2 tablespoons crème de menthe
2-1/2 cups powdered sugar, sifted

Chocolate Topping:
1 tablespoon water
A few drops vanilla extract
2 tablespoons unsalted butter
6 oz. semisweet chocolate, chopped

To make base, melt butter and corn syrup in a small saucepan; stir in cookies. Spread in bottom of an ungreased 13'' x 9'' baking pan; set aside. To make frosting, heat butter with whipping cream in a large bowl placed over a pan of gently simmering water, stirring until butter melts. Stir in crème de menthe and powdered sugar; beat until mixture thickens. Spread over base. Refrigerate 1 to 2 hours or until set.

To make topping, melt ingredients together in a small bowl placed over a pan of gently simmering water, stirring until smooth. Spread topping over frosting, covering it completely. Mark attractively with a spatula. Refrigerate until set; cut in 32 pieces.

Makes 32 cookies.

LIGHT BARS

2 Mars Bars candy, cut in small pieces
4 oz. semisweet chocolate, chopped
1/3 cup unsalted butter
3-2/3 cup puffed rice cereal

Grease a 13'' x 9'' baking pan with butter; line base with parchment or waxed paper. Melt Mars Bars, chocolate and butter in a large bowl placed over a pan of gently simmering water, stirring frequently until well blended and smooth. Remove from heat.

Add cereal to chocolate mixture; gently mix together until cereal is well coated. Spread evenly in prepared pan, smoothing top with the back of a spoon. Refrigerate 1 to 2 hours or until firmly set.

Using a very sharp knife, cut set cookie mixture in 24 pieces. Carefully remove bars from pan with a small flexible spatula. Store in an airtight container in a cool place for 3 to 4 days.

Makes 24 bars.

—— DATE & GINGER FANS ——

1/4 cup unsalted butter
2 tablespoons light corn syrup
4 oz. semisweet chocolate, chopped
6 oz. graham crackers, crushed
1/2 cup (3 oz.) pitted dates, chopped
1/3 cup (2 oz.) preserved stem ginger, chopped

To Finish:
Sifted powdered sugar for sprinkling

Melt butter, corn syrup and chocolate in a large bowl placed over a pan of gently simmering water, stirring frequently until well blended.

Add graham crackers, dates and ginger to chocolate mixture. Mix thoroughly. Spread evenly in a 9-inch-fluted flan pan with removable bottom, smoothing with the back of a spoon. Refrigerate 1 to 2 hours or until firm.

Carefully remove side from pan. Cut mixture in even-sized, triangle-shaped pieces. Using a spatula, carefully loosen cookies from base of pan, sprinkle with powdered sugar, then arrange neatly on a serving plate. Keep refrigerated, or in a cool place, until serving. Can be stored in an airtight container in a cool place for 2 to 3 days.

Makes about 16 cookies.

WHISKEY MACKS

1/4 cup unsweetened cocoa
2 tablespoons light corn syrup
1/4 cup whiskey
1/3 cup unsalted butter
8 oz. gingersnaps, finely crushed
1 cup (4 oz.) walnut pieces, chopped

To Finish:
Sifted powdered sugar for sprinkling

Line a large baking sheet with foil. Put cocoa, corn syrup, whiskey and butter in a medium-size saucepan; stir over low heat until melted and well blended. Remove from heat.

Stir gingersnaps and walnuts into whiskey mixture; allow to cool slightly. Roll pieces of mixture into balls about the size of a walnut, then flatten into even rounds. Place on prepared baking sheet. Refrigerate 1 to 2 hours or until firm.

Sprinkle powdered sugar lightly over cookies. Remove cookies from foil and arrange on a serving plate. Store in an airtight container in a cool place for 4 to 5 days.

Makes about 32 cookies.

—————— CALYPSO BARS ——————

8 oz. white chocolate, chopped
1/3 cup unsalted butter
1/4 cup dark rum
1/2 cup pistachio nuts
1/3 cup candied cherries, roughly chopped
1-1/3 cups (4 oz.) finely shredded coconut
1 oz. semisweet chocolate, melted

Grease a shallow 11'' x 7'' baking pan with butter; line base with parchment or waxed paper.

Heat white chocolate, butter and half of rum together in a large bowl placed over a pan of gently simmering water, stirring until well blended. Remove from heat; stir in remaining rum. Roughly chop pistachio nuts; add 3/4 of nuts to chocolate mixture with cherries and coconut. Mix well. Spread mixture evenly in prepared pan.

Finely chop remaining nuts. Put melted semi-sweet chocolate in a small paper piping bag; cut a small hole in bottom of bag. Pipe squiggly lines of chocolate all over top of mixture, then sprinkle with finely chopped nuts. Chill 4 to 5 hours or until firmly set. Cut in 30 pieces. Remove from pan with a flexible spatula. Keep refrigerated or in a cool place until serving.

Makes 30 bars.

GINGERSNAPS

1/3 cup unsalted butter
1/2 cup packed brown sugar
1/4 cup light corn syrup
1/4 cup black molasses
2 cups self-rising flour
1 teaspoon baking soda
2 teaspoons ground ginger
1 teaspoon ground allspice

Preheat oven to 350F (175C). Grease 2 baking sheets with butter. Put butter, sugar, corn syrup and molasses in a small saucepan; stir over low heat until butter is melted. Cool slightly.

Sift flour, baking soda, ginger and allspice into a medium-size bowl; make a well in the center and pour in syrup mixture. Mix to form a soft dough. Shape into walnut-size balls and place on prepared baking sheets, spacing well apart. Flatten each ball to form even rounds. Bake 15 minutes or until very lightly browned.

Remove Gingersnaps from oven, allow to cool 2 to 3 minutes on baking sheets then remove to a wire rack to cool completely. As the Gingersnaps cool they will become very crisp. Store in an airtight container in a cool place for 2 to 3 days.

Makes about 30 Gingersnaps.

—————— TUILLES ——————

1/4 cup unsalted butter
Finely grated peel of 1 medium-size orange
2 teaspoons Grand Marnier
2 egg whites
2/3 cup powdered sugar, sifted
1/2 cup all-purpose flour, sifted
1/3 cup (2 oz.) blanched almonds, halved and
   cut in thin slivers

To Finish:
Sifted powdered sugar for sprinkling

Preheat oven to 450F (230C). Grease several baking sheets with butter.

In a small saucepan, melt butter; stir in orange peel and Grand Marnier. Set aside to cool. In a medium-size bowl beat egg whites until soft peaks form; beat in powdered sugar. Fold in flour, then butter mixture. Mix almonds into batter. Drop small teaspoonfuls of mixture onto prepared baking sheets, spacing well apart. Using a fork dipped in cold water, flatten each mound to make a thin round. Bake in batches 5 minutes or until lightly browned around edges.

Once the cookies are removed from the oven, quickly place them over a rolling pin to give them a gently curved shape. Sprinkle with powdered sugar.

Makes about 30 Tuilles.

CHOCOLATE CRISPS

1/4 cup unsalted butter, softened
1/2 cup powdered sugar, sifted
1 teaspoon vanilla extract
3 egg whites, beaten
1/2 cup all-purpose flour, sifted
2 tablespoons unsalted butter, melted, cooled

To Finish:
4 oz. semisweet chocolate, chopped
1/3 cup finely shredded coconut

Preheat oven to 425F (220C). Grease several baking sheets with butter.

In a medium-size bowl beat 1/4 cup butter with powdered sugar until creamy; beat in vanilla. Gradually beat in egg whites. Fold in flour, then 2 tablespoons melted butter. Drop small teaspoonfuls of mixture onto prepared baking sheets, spacing well apart; flatten each teaspoonful slightly. Bake about 8 minutes or until lightly browned around edges. Using a spatula, immediately remove cookies from baking sheet to a wire rack; cool.

Melt chocolate in a small bowl placed over a pan of hot, but not boiling, water. When cookies are cool, spread each one with a thin layer of melted chocolate; allow chocolate to set slightly then sprinkle with coconut. Place in a cool place until chocolate sets completely.

Makes about 48 cookies.

FLORENTINES

1/4 cup unsalted butter
1/3 cup whipping cream
1/2 cup packed brown sugar
Finely grated peel of 1 large lemon
2 teaspoons lemon juice
1/4 cup all-purpose flour, sifted
1/2 cup (3 oz.) blanched almonds, slivered
1/2 cup chopped mixed citrus peel
1/3 cup candied cherries, chopped
1 oz. angelica, chopped
2 tablespoons golden raisins
1 oz. dried apricots, chopped
6 oz. semisweet chocolate, chopped

Preheat oven to 350F (175C). Grease several large baking sheets; line with parchment or waxed paper. Put butter, whipping cream, sugar, lemon peel and lemon juice in a large saucepan; stir over medium heat until butter melts. Remove from heat; stir in flour, almonds and fruit. Drop teaspoonfuls of mixture onto prepared baking sheets, spacing well apart. Using a fork dipped in cold water, flatten each teaspoonful into a circle about 2-1/2 inches in diameter.

Bake 10 to 12 minutes or until lightly browned around edges. Cool on baking sheets for a few minutes then remove with a spatula to wire racks; cool completely. Melt chocolate in a small bowl placed over a pan of hot, but not boiling, water. Taking one Florentine at a time, spread flat side with chocolate. Using a fork, mark chocolate with wavy lines. Place on a plate, chocolate-side-up, and leave to set.

Makes about 28 Florentines.

BRANDY SNAPS

1/2 cup butter
3/4 cup packed brown sugar
1/3 cup light corn syrup
4 teaspoons lemon juice
4 teaspoons brandy
1 cup all-purpose flour
1 teaspoon ground ginger

Put butter, sugar, corn syrup, lemon juice and brandy in a medium-size saucepan; stir over medium heat until butter melts and sugar dissolves. Remove from heat; sift flour and ginger into saucepan. Mix well. Allow mixture to cool completely.

Preheat oven to 375F (190C). Grease several baking sheets; line with parchment or waxed paper. For ease of handling, bake only 6 Brandy Snaps at a time, placing baking sheets in oven at 5 minute intervals. Parchment paper may be reused; wipe with a paper towel before spooning on more mixture. Drop small teaspoonfuls of mixture onto prepared baking sheets, spacing well apart. Bake 8 to 10 minutes or until very lightly browned. Have 6 wooden spoon handles or chopsticks ready to use for shaping cookies.

Allow Brandy Snaps to cool on the baking sheet for a few seconds. Remove with a spatula and wrap around handles of wooden spoons or chopsticks. When cookies are set, slide off of spoon handle or chopstick and place on a plate. If Brandy Snaps become too stiff to roll up, simply reheat for a few seconds to soften.

Makes about 36 Brandy Snaps.

——— AMERICAN HERMITS ———

1/2 cup butter, softened
1 cup packed brown sugar
1 egg, beaten
1/4 cup dairy sour cream
1/4 cup milk
2 cups all-purpose flour
2 teaspoons baking powder
Pinch of salt
1 teaspoon ground cinnamon
1/4 teaspoon ground nutmeg
1/4 teaspoon ground cloves
1 cup (6 oz.) raisins

Glaze:
3/4 cup powdered sugar, sifted
2 tablespoons half and half
A few drops vanilla extract

Preheat oven to 350F (175C). Grease several baking sheets with butter and dust with flour. In a large bowl, beat butter with brown sugar until very creamy. Beat in egg, sour cream and milk. Sift flour, baking powder, salt and allspice into bowl; mix well. Stir in raisins. Drop heaping teaspoonfuls of mixture onto prepared baking sheets, spacing well apart. Using a fork dipped in cold water, flatten each teaspoonful slightly. Bake about 15 minutes or until lightly browned.

Meanwhile, prepare glaze. In a small bowl, beat together powdered sugar, half and half and vanilla until smooth. As soon as the cookies come out of the oven, brush a thin layer of glaze over each one. Place on a wire rack to cool.

Makes about 36 cookies.

—— MADELEINES ——

4 eggs
3/4 cup sugar
1/2 teaspoon vanilla extract
1/2 teaspoon orange flower water
1-1/2 cups all-purpose flour
1/2 cup unsalted butter, melted, cooled

To Finish:
Superfine sugar for sprinkling

Preheat oven to 400F (205C). Grease 1 or 2 madeleine molds with melted butter and dust with flour.

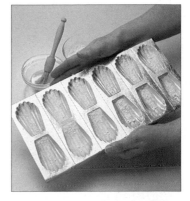

Put eggs, sugar, vanilla and orange flower water in a medium-size bowl. Place over a pan of gently simmering water; beat until very thick. Remove from heat. Continue beating until cool and the mixture retains its shape for a few seconds after a spoon is drawn through it. Carefully fold in flour; then gently fold in 1/2 cup melted butter.

Fill each madeleine mold 3/4 full with mixture. Bake 12 to 15 minutes or until lightly browned and springy to the touch. Remove from pans onto a wire rack, patterned-side-up. Sprinkle with superfine sugar immediately. Continue to bake Madeleines, in batches, until all mixture is used.

Makes about 42 Madeleines.

—————— PETIT LEMON CUPS ——————

2 tablespoons unsalted butter
5 teaspoons sugar
1 tablespoon light corn syrup
Finely grated peel of 1/2 a lemon
1/4 cup all-purpose flour, sifted

Filling:
3 tablespoons unsalted butter
Finely grated peel of 1 lemon
1 tablespoon lemon juice
1 tablespoon dairy sour cream
1-1/2 cups powdered sugar, sifted

Put butter, sugar, corn syrup and lemon peel in a small saucepan and stir over medium heat until melted. Stir in flour. Set aside to cool.

Preheat oven to 375F (190C). Grease a large baking sheet; line with parchment or waxed paper. Using a round 1/4 teaspoon measuring spoon, spoon 12 tiny circles of mixture onto prepared baking sheet, spacing well apart. Bake 5 minutes or until lightly browned. Cool a few seconds. Lift rounds from baking sheet and place in miniature tart pans to mold into a cup shape. When cool, remove to a wire rack. Repeat until mixture is all used.

To make filling, place butter, lemon peel and juice in a small bowl set over a pan of gently simmering water; stir until butter melts. Remove from heat. Stir in sour cream and powdered sugar. Beat until cool and thickened. Spoon or pipe filling into center of each cup.

Makes about 40 cups.

ITALIAN COOKIES

2 eggs
2/3 cup sugar
Finely grated peel of 1 lemon
1 cup all-purpose flour, sifted
1/2 cup (2 oz.) pine nuts
1/3 to 1/2 cup powdered sugar

Grease several baking sheets; line with parchment or waxed paper. Put eggs, sugar and lemon peel in a small bowl. Place over a pan of gently simmering water; beat until very thick. Remove from heat. Continue beating until cool and the mixture retains its shape for a few seconds after spoon is drawn through it. Fold in flour.

Drop teaspoonfuls of mixture onto prepared baking sheets, spacing well apart; sprinkle with pine nuts. Let stand 15 minutes. Meanwhile, preheat oven to 350F (175C).

Sprinkle powdered sugar evenly over cookies. Bake about 15 minutes or until lightly browned. Let cool on baking sheets a few minutes, then remove to wire racks to cool completely. Store in an airtight container in a cool place for 3 to 4 days.

Makes about 44 cookies.

EGGNOG BROWNIES

2 eggs
1 tablespoon brandy
1 teaspoon vanilla extract
1/2 cup butter
4 oz. unsweetened chocolate
1 cup sugar
1-1/3 cups packed brown sugar
1-1/4 cups all-purpose flour
1 cup (4 oz.) pecans, chopped

Grease a shallow 11'' x 7'' baking pan with butter; line base with parchment or waxed paper. Preheat oven to 350F (175C).

In a small bowl, lightly beat eggs with brandy and vanilla; set aside. Put butter and chocolate in a large saucepan; stir continuously over a medium heat until melted. Remove from heat; stir in sugars, flour, pecans and egg mixture. Pour into prepared pan; spread evenly. Bake 30 minutes or until a wooden pick inserted into the center comes out clean.

Allow brownies to cool in pan. When cool, cut in 24 squares. Remove from pan with a small flexible spatula. Brownies will keep well for up to a week stored in an airtight container in a cool place. These brownies taste better when they have sat for 2 to 3 days.

Makes 24 brownies.

APPLE STREUSEL BARS

Base:
1-1/4 cups all-purpose flour
1/2 cup powdered sugar
1-1/4 cups ground almonds
1 cup butter
3 rounded tablespoons lemon curd

Streusel Topping:
1 large red apple
1/3 cup packed brown sugar
1/3 cup butter, softened
1-1/2 cups all-purpose flour, sifted
1 teaspoon ground allspice

To Finish:
Sugar for sprinkling

Preheat oven to 350F (175C). To make base, sift flour and powdered sugar into a medium-size bowl. Mix in almonds. Cut in butter with a pastry blender until mixture resembles coarse crumbs. Mix together gently to form a soft dough. Roll out on a floured surface to a rect-angle slightly smaller than a 13'' x 9'' baking pan. Place rolled-out dough in pan and press to fit. Smooth top; prick well. Spread lemon curd over base. Refrigerate while making Streusel Topping.

To make topping, coarsely grate apple; squeeze dry using paper towels. Put in a small bowl with a little of the brown sugar; mix to separate strands. In a separate bowl, cut butter into flour until mixture resembles fine bread crumbs. Mix in allspice, apple and remaining brown sugar. Sprinkle evenly over lemon curd, pressing light-ly into curd. Bake 45 to 50 minutes or until lightly browned. Cool in pan. When cool, cut in 30 pieces. Sprinkle with sugar.

Makes 30 bars.

LEMON SHORTIES

Base:
1 cup butter, softened
1/2 cup powdered sugar, sifted
2 cups all-purpose flour
1/3 cup potato flour

Lemon Topping:
Finely grated peel of 3 lemons
1 cup sugar
3 eggs
1/2 cup all-purpose flour, sifted
3/4 teaspoon baking powder
3 tablespoons strained lemon juice

To Finish:
Powdered sugar for sprinkling

To make base, beat butter and powdered sugar together in a large bowl until creamy. Sift all-purpose flour and potato flour into bowl; mix into butter to form a soft dough. Spread evenly in base of an ungreased 13'' x 9'' baking pan. Cover surface with plastic wrap; rub with the back of a spoon to smooth. Remove plastic wrap; prick well. Chill 30 minutes. Meanwhile, preheat oven to 350F (175C). Bake about 15 minutes or until lightly browned. Remove from oven and set aside.

To make topping, put lemon peel, sugar and eggs in a medium-size bowl. Beat together until smooth and creamy. Sift flour and baking powder into bowl; fold into egg mixture. Stir in lemon juice. Pour Lemon Topping over base; return to oven 25 minutes or until very lightly browned. Cool in pan. When cool, cut in 30 bars. Sprinkle powdered sugar evenly over top.

Makes 30 Lemon Shorties.

NUTTY ORANGE BARS

3/4 cup butter
1/3 cup sugar
1/4 cup molasses
Finely grated peel of 1 large orange
2-3/4 cups rolled oats
1 cup walnuts, chopped

Preheat oven to 400F (205C). Grease a shallow 11'' x 7'' baking pan with butter. Put butter, sugar, molasses and orange peel in a large saucepan; stir continuously over medium heat until melted. Remove from heat.

Stir rolled oats and walnuts into melted mixture; spoon into prepared pan and smooth top. Bake about 20 minutes or until lightly browned. Remove from oven; cool 5 minutes then use a knife to mark lines on the mixture to use as a guide for cutting. Leave in pan until completely cool.

Loosen mixture from pan by running the tip of a knife around the inside edges of pan. Carefully turn mixture out onto a board. Cut through marked lines. These bars will keep well, for up to a week, stored in an airtight container in a cool place.

Makes 20 bars.

LINZERTORTE FINGERS

1-1/2 cups (8 oz.) unblanched almonds
2-1/2 cups all-purpose flour
Pinch of salt
1 teaspoon ground allspice
1 cup powdered sugar
Finely grated peel of 1 large lemon
1-1/4 cups unsalted butter, cut in small pieces
3 egg yolks
1 (12-oz.) jar raspberry jam
1 egg
2 teaspoons milk
2 teaspoons sugar
1/2 cup (2 oz.) flaked almonds

Finely grind unblanched almonds in a food processor or blender; place in a large bowl. Sift flour, salt, allspice and powdered sugar into bowl. Add lemon peel; mix well. Make a well in the center of flour and add butter and egg yolks; mix ingredients together to form a soft dough. Knead lightly until smooth. Cover bowl with plastic wrap and refrigerate 30 minutes. Preheat oven to 400F (205C).

Divide dough in half. Roll out one piece on a well-floured surface to fit a 13'' x 9'' baking pan; place in pan. Spread jam over pastry. Roll out other half of dough to fit pan; place on top of jam. Lightly beat egg with milk and sugar; brush pastry with glaze and sprinkle with flaked almonds. Bake 10 minutes; reduce temperature to 350F (175C). Bake 35 minutes longer or until golden. Cool in pan. When cold, cut in 30 pieces.

Makes 30 fingers.

FRUIT BARS

3/4 cup butter
1/4 cup packed brown sugar
1/4 cup light corn syrup
2-3/4 cups rolled oats
2/3 cup (3 oz.) dried apricots, chopped
1/2 cup (3 oz.) pitted dates, chopped
1/2 cup (3 oz.) pitted prunes, chopped

Preheat oven to 400F (205C). Grease a shallow 11'' x 7'' baking pan with butter. Put butter, sugar and corn syrup in a large saucepan; stir continuously over medium heat until melted. Remove from heat.

Stir rolled oats into melted mixture. Spread half of mixture in bottom of pan to form a thin layer. Press with the back of a spoon to compact the mixture and smooth the top. In a medium-size bowl, mix apricots, dates and prunes together. Sprinkle evenly over top of packed mixture. Spread remaining mixture on top of fruit; press with spoon again.

Bake about 20 minutes or until lightly browned. Cool 5 minutes. Using a knife, mark surface of mixture with lines to use as a guide for cutting. Leave in pan to cool completely. Cut in squares, then lift out with a small spatula. Store in an airtight container in a cool place for up to 1 week.

Makes 24 bars.

—— MARBLED SHORTBREAD ——

Shortbread:
2 cups all-purpose flour
Pinch of salt
1/4 cup sugar
3/4 cup butter, softened

Caramel:
1/2 cup unsalted butter
1 (14-oz.) can condensed milk
2 teaspoons instant coffee granules
1/4 cup sugar
2 tablespoons light corn syrup

Topping:
6 oz. semisweet chocolate, melted
1 oz. white chocolate, melted

Preheat oven to 350F (175C). To make shortbread, sift flour, salt and sugar into a medium-
size bowl. Cut in butter until mixture forms
coarse crumbs; mix together to form a soft
dough. Roll out dough on a floured surface to a
rectangle slightly smaller than a 13'' x 9'' baking pan. Place in pan; press to fit. Prick well.
Chill 30 minutes. Bake about 25 minutes or until
lightly browned; cool.

To make caramel, place all ingredients in a
heavy saucepan. Stir over medium heat until
butter melts. Continuing to stir, bring to a gentle
boil; boil 6 to 8 minutes or until mixture retains
its shape for a few seconds after a spoon is
drawn through it. Spread over shortbread; cool.
Spread semisweet chocolate over caramel.
Spoon melted white chocolate into a paper piping bag and cut a small hole in bag. Pipe lines
across semisweet chocolate, 1/2 inch apart. Pull
a metal skewer through lines to create marbling.
Allow chocolate to set. Cut in 48 squares.

Makes 48 small squares.

——CHOCOLATE-RAISIN BARS ——

1-3/4 cups all-purpose flour
Pinch of salt
8 teaspoons potato flour
1/4 cup vanilla sugar
3/4 cup butter
1/3 cup (2 oz.) raisins, chopped
8 oz. semisweet chocolate pieces

Preheat oven to 350F (175C). Sift all-purpose flour, salt, potato flour and vanilla sugar into a medium-size bowl. Cut in butter until mixture forms coarse crumbs; mix in raisins. Mix together to form a soft dough.

Roll out dough on a floured surface to a rectangle slightly smaller than an 11'' x 7'' baking pan. Place rolled-out dough in pan; press to fit. Smooth top; prick well. Bake about 25 minutes or until very lightly browned. Cool a few minutes. Using a sharp knife, mark through surface of mixture with lines to use as a guide for cutting. Let cool in pan.

Cut mixture in 20 squares; remove from pan. Place chocolate in a small bowl over a pan of gently simmering water; stir until melted and smooth. Line a baking sheet with foil. Dip bars in chocolate, coating evenly; lift out with a fork and tap gently on side of bowl to remove excess chocolate. Place on foil. Place baking sheet in a cool place until chocolate sets. If desired, any remaining chocolate can be piped over bars for decoration.

Makes 20 bars.

— CHERRY PRALINE RINGS —

1/2 cup (2 oz.) hazelnuts
2/3 cup sugar
1/2 cup butter, softened
1 egg
3 cups all-purpose flour
Pinch of salt
1 teaspoon baking powder
1 cup candied cherries, halved and thinly sliced

Glaze:
1 small egg, beaten
1 tablespoon milk
2 teaspoons sugar

To Finish:
Sugar for sprinkling

Lightly grease a small baking sheet. Put hazelnuts and 1/4 cup of the sugar in a small saucepan; stir over low heat until sugar caramelizes. Pour onto baking sheet; cool. Break into rough pieces and grind finely in a food processor or blender. Preheat oven to 350F (175C). Grease several baking sheets with butter. In a large bowl, cream butter with remaining sugar; beat in egg then praline. Sift flour, salt and baking powder into bowl; blend in with a spoon then mix with your hand to form a dough. Knead lightly to make a smooth dough.

Roll out dough on a floured surface to 1/8-inch thickness. Using a round 2-1/2-inch-fluted cookie cutter, cut out circles from dough; remove centers from circles with a round 1/2-inch-fluted cookie cutter. Place circles, slightly apart, on prepared baking sheets. Knead and roll out trimmings; cut out more circles. Mix all ingredients for glaze together; brush over circles. Decorate with candied cherries. Bake about 15 minutes or until lightly browned; sprinkle with sugar. Remove to wire racks; cool.

Makes 38 to 40 cookies.

— SHREWSBURY COOKIES —

2/3 cup butter, softened
2/3 cup sugar
1 egg
1 teaspoon vanilla extract
3 cups all-purpose flour
1 teaspoon baking powder
Pinch of salt

In a large bowl, beat butter with sugar until creamy. Beat in egg and vanilla. Sift flour, baking powder and salt into bowl; blend in with a spoon then mix with your hand to form a dough. Knead lightly to make a smooth dough.

Wrap dough in plastic wrap or waxed paper. Chill 45 minutes. Grease several baking sheets with butter. Roll out dough on a floured surface to 1/8-inch thickness. Using a round 2-1/2-inch-fluted cookie cutter, cut out circles from dough. Place circles, slightly apart, on prepared baking sheets. Knead and roll out trimmings; cut out more circles. Refrigerate unbaked 30 minutes. Preheat oven to 350F (175C).

Bake cookies about 15 minutes or until very lightly browned. Using a spatula, carefully remove cookies from baking sheets to wire racks; cool. Store in an airtight container.

Makes about 44 cookies.

SABLÉS

1-1/4 cups all-purpose flour
Pinch of salt
1/4 cup sugar
1/2 cup (2 oz.) finely ground almonds
Finely grated peel of 1 lemon
1/3 cup butter, softened
2 egg yolks

To Finish:
Sifted powdered sugar for sprinkling

Grease several baking sheets with butter. Stir flour, salt and sugar in a medium-size bowl; mix in almonds and lemon peel. Cut in butter until mixture resembles fine bread crumbs. Add egg yolks and mix to form a soft dough.

Roll out dough on a floured surface to 1/8-inch thickness. Using a rolling cookie cutter, cut rectangles from dough. Place, slightly apart, on prepared baking sheets. Refrigerate unbaked 30 minutes. Alternatively, cut cookies by hand with a knife or pastry wheel, cutting in 3'' x 1-3/4'' strips. Preheat oven to 350F (175C).

Bake Sablés about 15 minutes or until very lightly browned. Using a spatula, carefully remove cookies from baking sheets to wire racks; cool. When cool, sprinkle very lightly with powdered sugar. Store in an airtight container.

Makes about 32 cookies.

—— SUGAR & SPICE COOKIES ——

2 cups all-purpose flour
Pinch of salt
1/2 teaspoon ground cinnamon
1/4 teaspoon ground allspice
1/4 teaspoon ground mace
1/4 teaspoon ground cloves
1/2 teaspoon baking powder
1/2 cup sugar
1/2 cup butter, softened
1 egg, beaten
About 3 teaspoons water, if needed

Glaze:
1 small egg, beaten
1 tablespoon milk
2 teaspoons superfine sugar
2 tablespoons granulated sugar

Grease several baking sheets with butter. Stir flour, salt, spices, baking powder and sugar together in a medium-size bowl. Cut in butter until mixture resembles fine bread crumbs. Stir in egg then mix with your hand to form a soft dough. If dough is not soft, add water, 1 teaspoon at a time, until dough softens. Roll out dough on a floured surface to 1/8-inch thickness. Using fancy cookie cutters, cut out shapes from dough. Place on prepared baking sheets. Knead and roll out trimmings; cut out more shapes. Refrigerate unbaked 30 minutes. Preheat oven to 350F (175C).

To make glaze, stir egg, milk and superfine sugar together in a small bowl. Brush glaze over each cookie. Use 1 tablespoon of granulated sugar for sprinkling over glazed cookies. Bake 12 to 15 minutes or until lightly browned. Remove from oven. Immediately sprinkle cookies with remaining granulated sugar. Using a spatula, carefully remove cookies to wire racks; cool. Store in an airtight container.

Makes about 32 cookies.

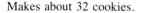

—— HAZELNUT SPECULAAS ——

2 cups (8 oz.) hazelnuts, lightly toasted,
    finely ground
1-1/4 cups (4 oz.) ground almonds
3/4 cup sugar
1 cup powdered sugar, sifted
2 teaspoons lemon juice
1 egg, beaten

Spicy Dough:
2 cups all-purpose flour
3/4 teaspoon baking powder
Pinch of salt
1 teaspoon ground allspice
1/2 cup packed brown sugar
1/2 cup butter, softened
2 small eggs
1 tablespoon milk
2 teaspoons sugar
20 blanched almonds, split in half

Put hazelnuts in a medium-size bowl with
almonds and sugars; mix well. Add lemon juice
and egg; mix to make a firm paste. On a surface
sprinkled with powdered sugar, knead paste until smooth. Divide in half; shape each piece into
a neat roll about 12 inches long. Wrap in plastic
wrap and chill.

To make dough, mix flour, baking powder, salt,
allspice and brown sugar in a medium-size
bowl; cut in butter until mixture resembles fine
bread crumbs. Mix in 1 beaten egg to form a
dough; knead lightly until smooth. Wrap in
plastic wrap; chill 30 minutes. Preheat oven to
350F (175C). Grease a large baking sheet with
butter.

Roll out dough on a lightly floured surface to a square slightly larger than 12 inches; trim edges to make straight. Cut square in half to make two (6-inch-wide) strips. Beat a second egg; brush over pastry strips. Place one roll of hazelnut paste on each strip; roll up neatly to enclose paste. Place rolls on prepared baking sheets, seam-side-down.

Mix remaining beaten egg with milk and sugar. Brush rolls with glaze. Decorate with almonds, placed slightly at an angle in a long line on top. Brush almonds with glaze.

Bake about 30 minutes or until golden. Using two large spatulas, very carefully remove rolls from baking sheet to a wire rack; cool. When cool, cut each roll diagonally in thin slices, cutting between almonds.

Makes about 40 Hazelnut Speculaas.

——— ALMOND FLOWERS ———

2-1/4 cups (8 oz.) ground almonds
1/2 cup sugar
3/4 cup powdered sugar, sifted
1 teaspoon rose water
1 teaspoon orange flower water
A few drops almond extract
3 egg yolks

Glaze:
1/4 cup sugar
1 tablespoon cool water
3 tablespoons warm water
2 egg yolks

To Decorate:
6 walnut halves, split in half
7 blanched almonds, split in half
8 pistachio nuts, split in half

In a medium-size bowl, mix ground almonds with sugars. Make a well in the center and add flavorings and egg yolks. Mix to form a stiff paste. Knead lightly until smooth. Wrap in plastic wrap. Set aside.

To make glaze, dissolve 1/4 cup sugar in cool water in a very small saucepan. Boil until caramelized. Add warm water; heat to dissolve caramelized sugar; cool. Beat in egg yolks. Preheat oven to 450F (230C). Line several baking sheets with parchment or waxed paper. Roll out almond paste to 1/4-inch thickness. Using a 2-inch flower-shaped cookie cutter, cut out flowers. Place on prepared baking sheets. Brush with glaze; decorate with nuts. Bake 5 minutes or until browned. Cool on baking sheets.

Makes about 42 flowers.

PINWHEELS

3/4 cup (12 tablespoons) butter, softened
3/4 cup (12 tablespoons) sugar
1 teaspoon vanilla extract
2 eggs
4-1/2 cups all-purpose flour
2 teaspoons baking powder
2 pinches of salt
2 tablespoons unsweetened cocoa
1 teaspoon brandy
1 egg white, very lightly beaten

Divide butter and sugar equally between 2 separate bowls.

To make vanilla dough, beat 1/2 of butter and sugar until creamy; beat in vanilla and 1 egg. Sift 1/2 of flour, 1/2 of baking powder and a pinch of salt into bowl. Blend in with a spoon then mix with your hand to form a dough. Wrap in plastic wrap; chill 45 minutes. Make chocolate dough in same way, using remaining butter, sugar, egg, flour, baking powder and salt, sifting cocoa in with remaining flour and baking powder. Add brandy to chocolate dough. Wrap and chill 45 minutes.

Roll out doughs separately on a floured surface to 13" x 11" rectangles. Brush vanilla dough with beaten egg white; place chocolate dough on top. Trim edges to make straight. Brush chocolate dough with egg white. Roll up, starting from one long side, to form a tight roll. Wrap in plastic wrap; chill 1 hour. Preheat oven to 350F (175C). Grease several baking sheets with butter. Cut roll in 1/4-inch-thick slices; place on prepared baking sheets. Bake 20 minutes or until lightly browned. Remove to wire racks; cool.

Makes about 48 Pinwheels.

CHOCOLATE PRETZELS

2 oz. unsweetened chocolate
1/2 cup butter, softened
1/2 cup sugar
1/2 teaspoon vanilla extract
1 egg
2-1/4 cups all-purpose flour
Pinch of salt
1/2 teaspoon baking powder
1 small egg white, lightly beaten
2 tablespoons demerara (brown) sugar

Melt chocolate in a small bowl placed over a pan of simmering water; cool.

In a medium-size bowl, beat butter with sugar until creamy; beat in vanilla, egg and melted chocolate. Sift flour, salt and baking powder into bowl. Blend in with a spoon then mix with your hand to form a smooth dough. Wrap in plastic wrap; chill 45 minutes. Grease several baking sheets with butter. Shape chilled dough into small walnut-size pieces.

To shape pretzels, roll each piece of dough into a thin strand about 11 inches long. Take each end, curve it around to form a loop, crossing ends over. Take ends back up to top of loop; press firmly to secure. Place on prepared baking sheets. Chill 30 minutes. Preheat oven to 350F (175C). Lightly brush pretzels with egg white; sprinkle with demerara sugar. Bake about 15 minutes. Carefully remove to wire racks; cool.

Makes about 42 pretzels.

GINGERBREAD MEN

4 cups all-purpose flour
Pinch of salt
2 teaspoons ground ginger
1 teaspoon ground allspice
2 teaspoons baking soda
1/2 cup butter
1/3 cup packed brown sugar
1/4 cup sugar
1/4 cup molasses
2 tablespoons light corn syrup
1 egg, beaten

Preheat oven to 350F (175C). Grease several baking sheets with butter. Sift dry ingredients into a large bowl; make a well in the center.

Put butter, sugars, molasses and corn syrup in a medium-size saucepan; stir over medium heat until butter melts. Pour mixture into well. Add beaten egg to well; mix to form a dough. On a floured surface, knead lightly to make smooth dough. Roll out dough to 1/8-inch thickness. Using a gingerbread man cookie cutter, cut men from dough. Place on prepared baking sheets. Knead and roll out trimmings; cut out more men. Continue until all dough is used.

Bake Gingerbread Men 12 to 15 minutes or until cookie springs back when lightly pressed. Cool on baking sheets a few minutes then remove to wire racks to cool completely. Traditionally, Gingerbread Men are left plain, but if desired they may be decorated as simply or elaborately as you choose, just let your imagination run wild! Royal icing, glacé icing and store-bought colored decorations are all suitable.

Makes about 24 Gingerbread Men depending on size of cutter.

OZNEI HAMAN

1/2 cup butter, softened
1/2 cup sugar
1 teaspoon vanilla extract
3 egg yolks
2 cups all-purpose flour
Pinch of salt
1 beaten egg for brushing

Poppy Seed Filling:
1/3 cup poppy seeds, finely ground
1 tablespoon honey
5 teaspoons sugar
Finely grated peel of 1/2 a lemon
1 tablespoon lemon juice
6 tablespoons ground almonds
1 small egg, beaten
1/4 cup (1 oz.) raisins

In a medium-size bowl, beat butter with sugar until creamy; beat in vanilla and egg yolks. Sift flour and salt into bowl; blend in with a spoon then mix with your hand to form a dough. Knead lightly until smooth. Wrap in plastic wrap and chill while making filling. To make filling, put poppy seeds, honey, sugar, lemon peel and juice in a small saucepan with 1/4 cup water. Bring to boil, stirring constantly.

Beat in almonds, beaten egg and raisins; cool. Preheat oven to 350F (175C). Grease 2 baking sheets with butter. Roll out dough on a floured surface to 1/8-inch thickness. Using a round 3-inch cookie cutter, cut out circles. Put a teaspoonful of mixture on each circle. Brush edges with beaten egg, bring edges to center to cover filling and form a triangle shape. Place on prepared baking sheets. Brush again with egg. Bake about 20 minutes. Remove to wire racks; cool.

Makes about 22 cookies.

LITTLE GEMS

1/3 cup butter, softened
1/3 cup powdered sugar, sifted
1 egg yolk
1 teaspoon vanilla extract
1 cup all-purpose flour
A pinch of salt

Icing:
1 egg white
1-1/2 cups powdered sugar, sifted
Food coloring, as desired

In a medium-size bowl, cream butter with powdered sugar; beat in egg yolk and vanilla. Sift
flour and salt into bowl; blend in with a spoon
then mix with your hand to form a smooth
dough. Wrap in plastic wrap; chill until firm.

Preheat oven to 350F (175C). Grease 2 large
baking sheets with butter. Roll out dough on a
floured surface to 1/8-inch thickness. Using a
round 3/4-inch-fluted cookie cutter, cut out
small circles. Place on prepared baking sheets.
Knead and roll out trimmings; cut out more
circles. Bake 8 to 10 minutes or until lightly browned. Remove from baking sheets to wire
racks; cool.

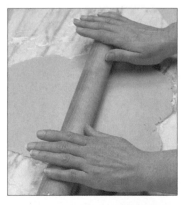

To make icing, lightly beat egg white in a small
bowl. Beat in powdered sugar until very white
and icing forms stiff peaks. Divide icing between three or four small bowls; color as desired. Spoon icings into small paper piping
bags, each one fitted with a small star tip. Pipe a
rosette of icing on each cookie. Let icing set.

Makes about 110 gems.

HARPTREE COOKIES

3/4 cup unsalted butter, softened
1/2 cup powdered sugar, sifted
Finely grated peel of 1 lemon
1-3/4 cups all-purpose flour
Pinch of salt

To Decorate, if desired:
5 to 6 candied cherries, cut in small pieces
80 small angelica leaves

To Finish:
Sifted powdered sugar for sprinkling

In a medium-size bowl, beat butter with powdered sugar until very light and fluffy; beat in lemon peel.

Sift flour and salt into bowl; mix in with your hand to form a soft dough. On a floured surface, knead lightly until smooth. Shape into a thick roll about 12 inches long. Wrap in plastic wrap; refrigerate 4 to 5 hours or overnight. Alternatively, store in refrigerator for up to 1 week before baking.

Preheat oven to 350F (175C). Grease several baking sheets with butter. Cut chilled dough diagonally in thin slices about 1/4 inch thick. Place slices on prepared baking sheets. If desired, decorate each cookie with a piece of candied cherry and angelica leaves. Bake about 15 minutes or until slightly browned. Cool on baking sheets a few minutes; remove to wire racks to cool completely. When cool, sprinkle lightly with powdered sugar.

Makes about 40 cookies.

MOCHA COOKIES

1-1/2 cups unsalted butter, softened
1-1/2 cups sugar
1 egg
1 teaspoon vanilla extract
1 teaspoon instant coffee granules dissolved in 2
**   teaspoons boiling water, then cooled**
1 oz. unsweetened chocolate, melted and cooled
3-3/4 cups all-purpose flour
Salt

In a medium-size bowl, beat butter with sugar until very light and fluffy. Beat in egg.

Divide creamed mixture evenly between 3 bowls. Beat vanilla into one bowl, cooled coffee into second bowl, and chocolate into third bowl. Sift 1-1/4 cups flour and a pinch of salt into each bowl. Blend into creamed mixtures with a spoon then mix with your hand to form a dough. On a floured surface, lightly knead doughs until smooth. Shape each one into a long smooth roll about 18 inches long.

Place vanilla and coffee rolls side by side. Place chocolate roll down center, on top. Press all three rolls together gently. Cut in half; wrap each piece in plastic wrap. Refrigerate 3 to 4 hours or overnight. Preheat oven to 350F (175C). Grease several baking sheets with butter. Cut chilled rolls in 1/4-inch-thick slices. Place on prepared baking sheets. Bake 15 to 18 minutes or until light brown. Remove from baking sheets to wire racks; cool.

Makes about 72 cookies.

—— JAMAICAN CRUNCHIES ——

1 cup unsalted butter, softened
1 cup packed light brown sugar
4 teaspoons rum
1-3/4 cups all-purpose flour
Pinch of salt
1/2 cup (2 oz.) ground almonds
1/2 cup (3 oz.) blanched almonds, lightly
    toasted, finely chopped
1 cup (3 oz.) finely shredded coconut

In a large bowl, beat butter with sugar until light and fluffy. Beat in rum. Sift flour and salt into bowl. Add ground and chopped almonds. Mix to form a dough.

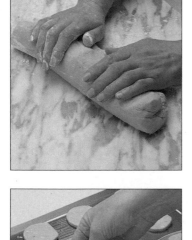

On a floured surface, lightly knead dough until smooth. Shape into a long smooth roll about 15 inches long. Wrap in plastic wrap; chill 3 to 4 hours or overnight. Preheat oven to 350F (175C). Grease several baking sheets with butter.

Cut chilled dough in 1/4-inch-thick slices. Place on prepared baking sheets. Sprinkle 2/3 of coconut evenly over cookies. Bake about 15 minutes or until very lightly browned. As soon as cookies are removed from oven, sprinkle with remaining coconut. Remove from baking sheets to wire racks; cool.

Makes about 60 cookies.

LANGUES DE CHAT

1/4 cup butter, softened
1/3 cup sugar
1 egg, beaten
1 teaspoon vanilla extract
1/2 cup all-purpose flour

Preheat oven to 425F (220C). Grease several baking sheets; line with parchment or waxed paper. In a medium-size bowl, beat butter with sugar until very light and fluffy. Gradually beat in egg and vanilla. Sift flour into bowl; fold in to form a soft dough.

Put dough in a piping bag fitted with a 3/8-inch-plain tip. Pipe 3-inch lengths of mixture onto prepared baking sheets, spacing well apart and cutting dough off at tip with a small knife when required length is reached.

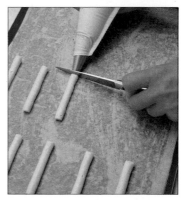

Bake 6 to 8 minutes or until golden brown around edges. Cool on baking sheets a few minutes. Using a spatula, very carefully remove cookies to a wire rack to cool completely.

Makes 36 to 40 cookies.

—— VIENNESE FINGERS ——

1 cup butter, softened
1/3 cup powdered sugar, sifted
1 teaspoon vanilla extract
2 cups all-purpose flour
Pinch of salt
1 tablespoon pistachio nuts, chopped

To Finish:
2 oz. semisweet chocolate pieces

Preheat oven to 350F (175C). Grease several baking sheets with butter; dust lightly with flour.

In a medium-size bowl, beat butter with powdered sugar until very light and creamy. Beat in vanilla. Sift flour and salt into bowl; mix into butter with a wooden spoon to form a soft dough. Put dough in a piping bag fitted with a 1/2-inch (10-point-star) tip. Pipe 2-1/2-inch lengths of mixture onto prepared baking sheets, spacing apart. Cut dough off at tip with a small knife when required length is reached. Sprinkle with pistachio nuts.

Bake about 20 minutes or until very lightly browned. Cool on baking sheets a few minutes then remove to wire racks to cool completely. Put chocolate in a small bowl and place over a pan of simmering water; stir until melted and smooth. Dip both ends of fingers in melted chocolate, scraping off excess on side of bowl; place on foil. Leave in a cool place until chocolate sets.

Makes about 24 cookies.

SHELL COOKIES

1 cup butter, softened
1/3 cup powdered sugar, sifted
1-3/4 cups all-purpose flour
Pinch of salt
3 tablespoons dry custard mix
15 candied cherries, cut in half

To Finish:
Sifted powdered sugar for sprinkling

Preheat oven to 350F (175C). Grease several baking sheets with butter; dust lightly with flour. In a medium-size bowl, beat butter with powdered sugar until very light and creamy. Sift flour, salt and custard mix into bowl; mix into butter with a wooden spoon to form a soft dough.

Put dough in a piping bag fitted with a 1/2-inch (10-point-star) tip. Pipe shell shapes onto pre-pared baking sheets, spacing well apart. Place half a candied cherry on pointed end of each shell.

Bake about 20 minutes or until very lightly browned. Cool on baking sheets a few minutes then remove to wire racks to cool completely. When cool, sprinkle powdered sugar lightly over cookies.

Makes about 30 cookies.

─────── VIENNESE WHIRLS ───────

3/4 cup unsalted butter, softened
3 tablespoons powdered sugar, sifted
1/2 teaspoon vanilla extract
1 teaspoon Grand Marnier
1-1/2 cups all-purpose flour
Pinch of salt

To Finish:
Sifted powdered sugar for sprinkling
2 teaspoons red jam

Preheat oven to 350F (175C). Place 12 paper baking cups in a muffin pan.

In a medium-size bowl, beat butter with powdered sugar until very light and fluffy. Beat in vanilla and Grand Marnier. Sift flour and salt into bowl; mix into butter with a wooden spoon to form a soft dough. Put dough in a piping bag fitted with a 1/2-inch (10-point-star) tip. Pipe a whirl of mixture into each paper cup, starting in the center of each cup and working outwards.

Bake about 20 minutes or until very lightly browned. Carefully remove to a wire rack; cool. When cool, sprinkle powdered sugar very lightly over each whirl. Spoon, or pipe, a small amount of jam into the center of each whirl.

Makes 12 to 16 Viennese Whirls.

——— CIGARETTES RUSSES ———

1/4 cup unsalted butter, softened
1/2 cup superfine sugar
1/2 teaspoon vanilla extract
3 egg whites
1/2 cup all-purpose flour
2 tablespoons melted butter, cooled

Preheat oven to 350F (175C). Grease several baking sheets with butter. Have 6 wooden spoon handles or chopsticks ready for shaping baked cookies.

In a medium-size bowl, beat butter with sugar until creamy. Beat in vanilla. Gradually beat in egg whites. Sift flour into bowl; stir into creamed mixture until smooth. Mix in cooled butter. Spoon mixture into a piping bag fitted with a 3/8-inch-plain tip. Pipe six mounds, about 1-1/2 inches in diameter, onto each prepared baking sheet, spacing very well apart. Spread each mound out thinly to a circle about 3 inches in diameter.

Bake 1 tray of mixture at a time for 5 to 6 minutes or until golden brown around edges. Remove from oven. Remove circles from baking sheet immediately with a spatula. Quickly roll each one around a wooden spoon handle or chopstick to shape; place on a wire rack to cool. Remove spoon handles or chopsticks as soon as cookies hold their shape. Repeat with remaining mixture.

Makes 28 to 30 cookies.

—— TRIPLE ORANGE DROPS ——

1/4 cup unsalted butter, softened
1/4 cup sugar
Finely grated peel of 1 small orange
1 teaspoon Grand Marnier
1 egg, beaten
1/2 cup all-purpose flour
1 tablespoon finely chopped candied orange peel

Glaze:
2 tablespoons orange marmalade, heated, sieved
1/3 cup powdered sugar, sifted
1 teaspoon Grand Marnier
2 teaspoons fresh orange juice

Preheat oven to 425F (220C). Grease 2 baking sheets with butter. In a medium-size bowl, beat butter with sugar and orange peel until creamy. Beat in 1 teaspoon Grand Marnier. Gradually beat in egg. Sift flour into bowl and add candied peel; stir until smooth. Put mixture in a piping bag fitted with a 1/2-inch-plain tip. Pipe circles of mixture, about 1-1/2 inch in diameter, onto prepared baking sheets, spacing well apart. Bake 6 to 8 minutes or until golden brown around edges and dry in center.

Meanwhile, prepare glaze. Heat marmalade in a small saucepan until boiling. In a small bowl, blend powdered sugar with Grand Marnier and orange juice to make a thin icing. As soon as cookies are removed from oven, brush each one first with marmalade and then with icing; glaze evenly. Return cookies to oven 30 seconds to set glaze. Using a spatula, very carefully remove cookies from baking sheets to wire racks; cool.

Makes about 24 Triple Orange Drops.

——— BRANDY SHAPES ———

1/2 cup butter, softened
3/4 cup sugar
2 teaspoons brandy
1 egg, beaten
2 cups all-purpose flour
Pinch of salt

To Decorate:
14 raisins
Sifted powdered sugar for sprinkling
1/3 cup powdered sugar, sifted
1 tablespoon lemon juice
Lemon-flavored fruit slices

Preheat oven to 375F (190C). Grease several baking sheets with butter. In a medium-size bowl, beat butter with sugar until very creamy.

Beat in brandy. Gradually beat in egg. Sift flour and salt into bowl; mix in with a wooden spoon to form a fairly stiff dough. Put mixture in a piping bag fitted with a 1/2-inch (10-point-star) tip. Pipe half of mixture onto prepared baking sheets in 2-inch-long "S" shapes, spacing well apart. Decorate with raisins. Pipe remaining mixture into rings.

Bake cookies about 15 minutes or until lightly browned. Remove from baking sheets to wire racks; cool. To decorate, sprinkle powdered sugar very lightly over "S" shapes. In a small bowl, blend 1/3 cup powdered sugar with lemon juice to make a thin icing. Brush over rings; decorate with fruit slices before icing sets.

Makes about 28 cookies.

CINNAMON FINGERS

2 egg whites
1-1/4 cups sugar
4 teaspoons potato flour
2 teaspoons ground cinnamon
1-2/3 cups (6 oz.) ground almonds
1/3 cup finely shredded coconut

Preheat oven to 350F (175C). Grease several baking sheets; line with parchment or waxed paper. In a medium-size bowl, beat egg whites until stiff peaks form. Add sugar, potato flour, cinnamon and ground almonds.

Mix together gently to form a stiff paste. Put in a piping bag fitted with a 3/8-inch-plain tip. Pipe 3-inch lengths of mixture onto prepared baking sheets, spacing well apart. Sprinkle evenly with coconut.

Bake 25 minutes or until lightly browned. Cool on baking sheets a few minutes then remove to wire racks to cool completely.

Makes about 40 cookies.

SPRITZ COOKIES

1 cup butter, softened
1-1/4 cups sugar
1 teaspoon vanilla extract
2 eggs
3-1/2 cups all-purpose flour
Pinch of salt

To Decorate, as desired:
Candied cherries, cut in small pieces
Angelica leaves
Candied fruit, cut in small pieces
Chopped nuts
Sugar or colored sugars
Powdered sugar

Preheat oven to 375F (190C). Lightly grease several baking sheets with butter. In a large bowl, beat butter with sugar until creamy; beat in vanilla and eggs. Sift flour and salt into bowl; mix in with a wooden spoon to form a fairly stiff dough. Shape dough, on a floured surface, into rolls. Place rolls, one at a time, in a cookie press and press out desired shapes onto prepared baking sheets.

Decorate cookies as desired with candied cherries, angelica leaves, candied fruits or nuts. Bake 12 to 15 minutes or until very lightly browned. Remove from baking sheets to wire racks. If desired, sprinkle cookies with sugar or colored sugars; cool. When cool, cookies can be sprinkled with powdered sugar, if desired.

Makes about 120 cookies.

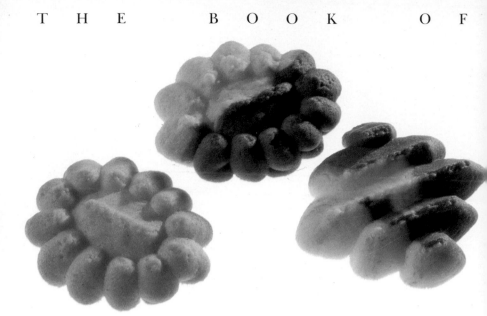

— FLAVORED SPRITZ COOKIES —

1/2 cup butter, softened
3/4 cup powdered sugar, sifted
Finely grated peel of 1 lemon
1 egg
2 cups all-purpose flour
Pinch of salt
2 teaspoons ground ginger
Water, if needed

Variation:
Finely grated peel of 1 medium-size orange
2 oz. unsweetened chocolate, melted and cooled
2 teaspoons ground allspice

Preheat oven to 375F (190C). Lightly grease several baking sheets with butter. In a medium-size bowl, beat butter with powdered sugar and lemon peel until creamy; beat in egg.

Sift flour, salt and ginger into bowl; mix in with a wooden spoon to form a fairly stiff dough. If dough is too stiff, add 1 teaspoon of water at a time until dough softens. Fill a cookie press with dough. Press out desired shapes onto prepared baking sheets. Bake 10 to 12 minutes or until very lightly browned. Remove from baking sheets to wire racks; cool.

Makes about 60 cookies.

For Variation: Orange peel may be creamed in with butter. Add melted chocolate after beating in egg. Sift allspice in with flour. Leave cookies plain or decorate as directed for Spritz Cookies on page 63. Two-tone cookies may be made by filling cookie press with both a plain dough and a chocolate dough. Place a roll of each mixture side by side in the cookie press.

-COCONUT-CARAMEL SANDWICH-

2 egg whites
3/4 cup sugar
4 teaspoons potato flour
2 cups (6 oz.) finely shredded coconut

Caramel Filling:
2 tablespoons unsalted butter
1 tablespoon light corn syrup
1/2 cup condensed milk
1/2 teaspoon vanilla extract

Preheat oven to 350F (175C). Grease several baking sheets; line with parchment or waxed paper.

In a small bowl, beat egg whites until stiff peaks form; fold in sugar, flour and coconut. Gently press mixture together to form a soft paste. Roll out to 1/4-inch thickness on a surface lightly sprinkled with sifted potato flour. Using a 2-inch-round cookie cutter, cut out circles. Place on prepared baking sheets, spacing well apart. Press trimmings together and roll out; cut out more circles. Continue until mixture is used up.

Bake about 20 minutes or until just lightly browned. Cool on baking sheets. To make filling, put ingredients in a small heavy saucepan and place over medium heat. Stir continuously until mixture thickens enough to retain its shape for a few seconds after a spoon is drawn through the mixture. Be careful not to let caramel burn. Sandwich cookies together with caramel.

Makes about 12 to 14 cookies.

–ORANGE & CHOCOLATE RINGS–

1/2 cup butter, softened
3/4 cup packed brown sugar
1 egg, beaten
2 cups all-purpose flour
1/2 teaspoon baking powder
Pinch of salt

To Coat:
6 oz. semisweet chocolate, melted

Filling:
3 tablespoons unsalted butter
3 tablespoons whipping cream
1 cup powdered sugar, sifted
Finely grated peel of 1 medium-size orange
1 tablespoon Grand Marnier

Preheat oven to 350F (175C). Grease several baking sheets with butter. In a medium-size bowl, beat butter with brown sugar until creamy; beat in egg. Sift dry ingredients into bowl; blend in with a spoon then mix with your hand to form a soft dough. Roll out dough on a floured surface to 1/8-inch thickness. Using a round 2-inch-fluted cookie cutter, cut out circles.

Place circles on prepared sheets. Remove centers with a 3/4-inch-round cookie cutter. Knead and roll out trimmings; cut out more circles.

Bake 15 minutes or until lightly browned. Remove to wire racks; cool. Coat half of rings with melted chocolate; place on foil or parchment paper until chocolate sets. To make filling, place butter and whipping cream in a bowl set over a pan of hot water; stir until butter melts. Remove from heat. Stir in powdered sugar, orange peel and Grand Marnier. Beat until mixture cools and thickens. Sandwich plain rings and chocolate rings together with filling.

Makes about 24 cookies.

—— VANILLA CREAMS ——

1/2 cup butter, softened
1/4 cup sugar
1 egg, beaten
1 teaspoon vanilla extract
1-3/4 cups all-purpose flour
3 tablespoons cornstarch
1/2 teaspoon baking powder
Pinch of salt

Vanilla Filling:
1/4 cup unsalted butter, softened
3/4 cup powdered sugar, sifted
1 egg yolk
1/2 teaspoon vanilla extract

To Finish:
Sifted powdered sugar for sprinkling

Preheat oven to 350F (175C). Grease several baking sheets with butter. In a medium-size bowl, beat butter with sugar until creamy; gradually beat in egg then vanilla. Sift dry ingredients into bowl; blend in with a spoon then mix with your hand to form a soft dough. Roll out dough on a floured surface to 1/8-inch thickness. Mark surface of dough with a ridged rolling pin.

Using a 2-inch flower-shaped cookie cutter, cut out flowers from dough; place on prepared baking sheets. Knead and roll out trimmings; cut out more flowers. Bake 15 minutes or until very lightly browned. Remove from baking sheets to wire racks; cool. To make filling, beat butter with sugar in a small bowl until creamy. Beat in egg yolk and vanilla. Sandwich cookies together with filling. Sprinkle very lightly with powdered sugar.

Makes about 24 cookies.

——— CHOCOLATE DREAMS ———

1/2 cup butter, softened
1/4 cup sugar
1 egg, beaten
1-3/4 cups all-purpose flour
1/4 cup unsweetened cocoa
1/2 teaspoon baking powder
Pinch of salt

Glaze:
1 tablespoon milk
2 teaspoons superfine sugar, plus a little extra
   for sprinkling

Chocolate Filling:
1/3 cup whipping cream
3 oz. semisweet chocolate, chopped

Preheat oven to 350F (175C). Grease several baking sheets with butter. In a medium-size bowl, beat butter with sugar until creamy; beat in egg. Sift flour, cocoa, baking powder and salt into bowl; blend in with a spoon, then mix with your hand to form a dough. Roll out dough on a floured surface to 1/8-inch thickness. Using fancy 2-inch cookie cutters, cut out shapes from dough as desired; place on prepared baking sheets. Knead and roll out trimmings; cut out more shapes.

To make glaze, stir milk and superfine sugar together in a small bowl until sugar dissolves. Brush over cookies. Bake 10 minutes. Sprinkle with extra sugar; cool on wire racks. To make filling, put whipping cream and chocolate in a small saucepan and stir over low heat until chocolate melts; do not boil. Pour into a small bowl. Cool until almost set then beat until fluffy. Sandwich cookies together with a generous amount of filling. Leave in a cool place until filling sets.

Makes about 30 cookies.

—— HONEY & LEMON CREAMS ——

2 cups self-rising flour
2 teaspoons baking soda
2 teaspoons ground allspice
1/4 cup sugar
1/2 cup butter, softened
1/3 cup clear honey

Lemon Cream:
1/4 cup unsalted butter, softened
3/4 cup powdered sugar, sifted
Finely grated peel of 1 lemon
1 egg yolk
1 tablespoon lemon juice

Preheat oven to 400F (205C). Grease several baking sheets; line with parchment or waxed paper. Put flour, baking soda, allspice and sugar in a medium-size bowl. Cut in butter until mixture resembles fine bread crumbs. In a small saucepan, heat honey until warm, but not hot. Pour into flour mixture; mix to form a dough. Shape dough into balls about the size of unshelled hazelnuts. Place on prepared baking sheets, spacing well apart.

Bake 8 to 10 minutes or until golden brown. Cool on baking sheets until firm then remove to wire racks to cool completely. To make Lemon Cream, beat butter with powdered sugar and lemon peel in a small bowl until creamy. Beat in egg yolk and lemon juice. Sandwich cookies together with Lemon Cream. Leave in a cool place until filling sets.

Makes about 28 cookies.

———— LIME CREAMS ————

1 recipe Vanilla Creams cookie dough (page 67)

Lime Filling:
1/4 cup unsalted butter, softened
3/4 cup powdered sugar, sifted
Very finely grated peel of 1 lime
4 teaspoons lime juice
Sifted powdered sugar for sprinkling

Glacé Icing:
1/4 cup powdered sugar, sifted
3-1/2 to 4 teaspoons lime juice
A few drops green food coloring

Preheat oven to 350F (175C). Grease several baking sheets with butter. Roll out cookie dough on a floured surface to 1/8-inch thickness. Using a round 2-1/4-inch-fluted cookie cutter, cut out circles from dough; place on prepared baking sheets. Remove centers from half of circles with a round 1-1/2-inch-plain cookie cutter. Knead and roll out trimmings; cut out more circles and rings, making sure to have an equal number of each. Bake 15 minutes or until lightly browned. Remove to wire racks; cool.

To make Lime Filling, beat butter with powdered sugar and lime peel in a small bowl until creamy. Beat in lime juice. Spread filling on whole circles; place rings on top. Lightly sprinkle powdered sugar over rings. To make Glacé Icing, blend 1/4 cup powdered sugar with lime juice and a few drops of green food coloring in a small bowl to make an icing thick enough to coat the back of a spoon. Fill center of rings with icing. Allow icing to set.

Makes about 22 to 24 cookies.

—— PASSION FRUIT CREAMS ——

**1 recipe Vanilla Creams cookie dough
(page 67), substituting finely grated peel
of 1 lemon for vanilla extract**

Filling:
**4 passion fruit
1/4 cup unsalted butter, softened
3/4 cup powdered sugar, sifted**

To Finish:
Sifted powdered sugar for sprinkling

Preheat oven to 350F (175C). Grease several baking sheets with butter. Roll out cookie dough on a floured surface to 1/8-inch thickness.

Using a 3-inch heart-shaped cookie cutter, cut out hearts from dough; place on prepared baking sheets. Knead and roll out trimmings; cut out more hearts. Bake 15 minutes or until very lightly browned. Remove from baking sheets to wire racks; cool.

To make filling, cut each passion fruit in half. Scoop out flesh into a nylon sieve placed over a small bowl. Work seeds against nylon with a spoon to extract juice, about 8 teaspoons. In another small bowl, beat butter with powdered sugar until creamy. Gradually beat in passion fruit juice. Sandwich hearts together with passion fruit filling. Sprinkle lightly with powdered sugar.

Makes about 22 cookies.

FILIGREE COOKIES

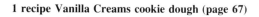

1 recipe Vanilla Creams cookie dough (page 67)

Filling:
2 tablespoons unsalted butter, softened
1/3 cup powdered sugar, sifted
A few drops vanilla extract

To Finish:
Sifted powdered sugar for sprinkling
1 tablespoon raspberry jam, sieved
1 tablespoon apricot jam, sieved
1 tablespoon lime marmalade, sieved

Preheat oven to 350F (175C). Grease several baking sheets with butter. Roll out dough on a floured surface to 1/8-inch thickness. Using a 3-inch (3-point-star) cookie cutter, cut out shapes from dough; place on prepared baking sheets. Using a 1-inch club-shaped cookie cutter, cut a small hole in each point of half of cookies. Knead and roll out trimmings; cut out more shapes. Half the cookies should be solid; the remaining half should be cut-outs. If you do not have these shaped cutters, use round fluted cookie cutters instead.

Bake 15 minutes or until lightly brown. Cool on wire racks. To make filling, beat butter with powdered sugar and vanilla in a small bowl until creamy. Spread over solid cookies; place cut-out cookies on top. Sprinkle lightly with powdered sugar. Put each jam in a separate small paper piping bag. Cut a small hole in bottom of each. Pipe a different jam into the cut-out portion of each cookie.

Makes about 18 cookies.

VIENNESE CREAMS

1 recipe Viennese Fingers cookie dough (page 56), pistachio nuts and chocolate omitted

Filling:
1/2 cup unsalted butter, softened
3/4 cup powdered sugar, sifted
1 teaspoon vanilla extract
2 tablespoons very thick cold custard
1 to 2 tablespoons red jam

To Finish:
Sifted powdered sugar for sprinkling

Preheat oven to 350F (175C). Grease several baking sheets; dust lightly with flour.

Put cookie dough in a piping bag fitted with a 1/2-inch (12-point-star) tip. Pipe 32 (2-1/2-inch) lengths of mixture onto prepared baking sheets, spacing apart, cutting mixture off at tip with a small knife when required length is reached. Bake about 20 minutes or until lightly browned. Cool on trays a few minutes then remove to wire racks to cool completely.

To make filling, beat butter with powdered sugar in a medium-size bowl until creamy. Beat in vanilla. Gradually beat in custard. If necessary, refrigerate filling briefly to stiffen. Spoon filling into a piping bag fitted with same tip used to pipe cookie dough. Spread jam thinly on flat side of half the cookies, pipe a line of filling on top. Sandwich with remaining cookies; sprinkle lightly with powdered sugar. Keep cool until serving.

Makes about 16 cookies.

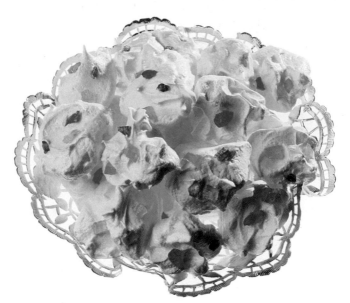

—— HARLEQUIN BUBBLES ——

2 egg whites
1/2 cup superfine sugar
1 tablespoon chopped mixed candied fruits

Grease several baking sheets; line with parchment or waxed paper. In a very clean grease-free bowl, beat egg whites until very stiff, but not dry. Add 1/2 tablespoon of the sugar; beat until sugar is incorporated and meringue is stiff and shiny. Add remaining sugar, a little at a time, beating well after each addition.

Preheat oven to 275F (135C). Using two small teaspoons, spoon very small mounds of meringue onto prepared baking sheets, spacing apart. Sprinkle each meringue with a few pieces of candied fruit.

Bake meringues 1-1/4 hours or until crisp and dry on the outside, but soft in the center; cool. Remove meringues from paper. Depending on the oven used, it may be necessary to select a slightly lower temperature to keep meringues white.

Makes about 36 meringues.

CHESTNUT MERINGUES

2 egg whites
1/2 cup superfine sugar
1 teaspoon vanilla extract
4 marrons glacés, chopped
2 teaspoons superfine sugar for sprinkling

To Finish:
1 teaspoon sweetened hot chocolate mix, sifted

Grease several baking sheets; line with parchment or waxed paper. Preheat oven to 275F (135C). In a very clean grease-free bowl, beat egg whites until very stiff, but not dry.

Add 1/2 tablespoon of the sugar; beat until sugar is incorporated and meringue is stiff and shiny. Add remaining sugar, a little at a time, beating well after each addition. Beat in vanilla. Carefully fold in chopped marrons glacés. Using two small teaspoons, spoon small oval shapes of mixture onto prepared baking sheets. Lightly sprinkle sugar over meringues.

Bake meringues 1-1/4 hours or until crisp and dry on outside, but soft in the center; cool. Sprinkle hot chocolate mix lightly over each meringue. Remove meringues from paper.

Makes about 36 meringues.

PISTACHIO RINGS

2 egg whites
1/2 cup superfine sugar
1 tablespoon pistachio nuts, finely chopped

Grease several baking sheets; line with parchment or waxed paper. Preheat oven to 275F (135C). Put egg whites and sugar in a clean grease-free bowl. Place bowl over a pan of gently simmering water; beat until mixture becomes thick and shiny. Do not overheat. Remove bowl from heat; continue to beat until stiff peaks form.

Spoon meringue into a piping bag fitted with a 1/2-inch (6-point-star) tip. Pipe small rings of meringue, about 2 inches in diameter, onto prepared baking sheets. Sprinkle pistachio nuts over each ring.

Bake meringues 1-1/2 hours or until dry; cool. Remove from paper. Depending on the oven used, it may be necessary to select a slightly lower temperature to keep meringues white.

Makes about 36 rings.

−WALNUT-CHOCOLATE COOKIES−

2 egg whites
3/4 cup superfine sugar
1-3/4 cups (6 oz.) walnuts, finely ground
3 oz. semisweet chocolate, finely grated
25 walnut halves, cut in half

Preheat oven to 350F (175C). Line several baking sheets with rice paper. In a medium-size bowl, beat egg whites until soft peaks form.

Very carefully fold sugar, ground walnuts and chocolate into egg whites until mixture is smooth. Spoon into a piping bag fitted with a 3/4-inch-plain tip. Pipe small circles, about 1-1/2 inches in diameter, on prepared baking sheets, spacing well apart.

Place a walnut quarter in the center of each circle. Bake 20 minutes. Remove from oven; leave cookies on baking sheets until cool. When cool, remove cookies and peel paper off each.

Makes about 50 cookies.

—— HAZELNUT COOKIES ——

2 egg whites
1-1/2 cups hazelnuts, finely ground
3/4 cup superfine sugar
Finely grated peel of 1 lemon
1/2 teaspoon ground cinnamon
10 candied cherries, cut in quarters

Preheat oven to 350F (175C). Line several baking sheets with rice paper. In a medium-size bowl, beat egg whites until soft peaks form.

Very carefully fold hazelnuts, sugar, lemon peel and cinnamon into egg whites until mixture is smooth. Spoon into a piping bag fitted with a 3/4-inch-plain tip. Pipe small circles, about 1-1/2 inches in diameter, onto prepared baking sheets, spacing well apart. Place a cherry quarter in the center of each circle.

Bake 20 minutes or until very lightly browned. Remove from oven; leave cookies on baking sheets until cool. When cool, remove cookies and peel paper off each one.

Makes about 40 cookies.

CAFÉ STERNEN

2 egg whites
1/2 cup superfine sugar
1 teaspoon coffee-flavored liqueur
28 pecans or walnuts, halved

To Finish:
3 oz. semisweet chocolate, chopped

Preheat oven to 275F (135C). Grease several baking sheets; line with parchment or waxed paper.

In a clean grease-free bowl, beat egg whites until very stiff, but not dry. Add 1/2 tablespoon of the sugar; beat until incorporated and meringue is stiff and shiny. Add remaining sugar, a little at a time, beating well after each addition. Beat in liqueur. Spoon mixture into a large piping bag fitted with a 1-inch (12-point-star) tip. Pipe stars onto prepared baking sheets. Press a pecan or walnut half into the center of each star.

Bake meringues 1-1/2 hours or until dry. Put chocolate in a small bowl and place over a pan of gently simmering water until melted. Remove bowl from heat and stir until smooth. Carefully remove meringues from paper. Dip base of each one about a 1/4 inch deep into the melted chocolate. Pull meringue across the back of a knife to remove excess chocolate. Place on parchment or waxed paper until chocolate sets.

Makes about 56 cookies.

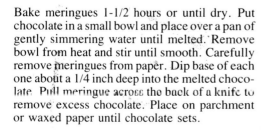

AMARETTI

1 egg white
2 teaspoons Amaretto
A few drops almond extract
1-2/3 cups (6 oz.) ground almonds
1-1/2 cups powdered sugar, sifted

To Finish:
Sifted powdered sugar for sprinkling

Preheat oven to 350F (175C). Grease several baking sheets; line with parchment or waxed paper. In a small bowl, very lightly beat egg white, Amaretto and almond extract together.

Put almonds and sugar in a large bowl and mix well. Make well in center. Pour egg white mixture into well; mix to form a paste.

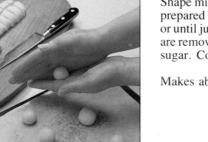

Shape mixture into 36 equal-size balls; place on prepared baking sheets. Bake about 15 minutes or until just lightly browned. As soon as cookies are removed from oven, sprinkle with powdered sugar. Cool Amaretti on baking sheets.

Makes about 36 Amaretti.

—— MERINGUE MUSHROOMS ——

2 egg whites
1/2 cup superfine sugar
1/2 teaspoon vanilla extract
2 oz. semisweet chocolate, melted

To Finish:
1 teaspoon unsweetened cocoa

Preheat oven to 275F (135C). Grease several baking sheets; line with parchment or waxed paper. In a clean grease-free bowl, beat egg whites until very stiff, but not dry. Add 1/2 tablespoon of the sugar; beat until incorporated and meringue is stiff and shiny.

Add remaining sugar, a little at a time, beating well after each addition. Beat in vanilla. Spoon mixture into a large piping bag fitted with a 1/2-inch-plain tip. To make mushroom caps, pipe 40 rounded mounds, about 1 inch in diameter, onto prepared baking sheets. To make stalks, pipe 40 pyramid-shaped blobs.

Bake 1 hour or until dry. Cool on baking sheets. Remove mushroom caps; cut a small hole in flat side of each one. Fill with a little melted chocolate. Insert pointed ends of stalks into chocolate. Leave mushrooms upside down until chocolate sets. Stand mushrooms upright and sprinkle lightly with cocoa. If desired, mushrooms may be made into "toadstools" by painting with dots of red food coloring.

Makes about 40 Meringue Mushrooms.

MINTY STICKS

2 egg whites
1/2 cup superfine sugar
1 teaspoon crème de menthe
2 oz. crisp mint-flavored chocolate sticks,
  finely chopped
2 teaspoons chocolate sprinkles

Preheat oven to 275F (135C). Grease several baking sheets; line with parchment or waxed paper.

In a clean grease-free bowl, beat egg whites until very stiff, but not dry. Add 1/2 tablespoon of the sugar; beat until incorporated and meringue is stiff and shiny. Add remaining sugar, a little at a time, beating well after each addition. Beat in crème de menthe; fold in chopped chocolate sticks.

Spoon meringue into a large piping bag fitted with a 1/2-inch-plain tip. Pipe 3-inch lengths of meringue onto prepared baking sheets. Decorate with chocolate sprinkles. Bake 1 hour or until dry. Cool on baking sheets then carefully remove from paper. Store in an airtight container.

Makes about 56 Minty Sticks.

—— JAPONAIS SANDWICHES ——

2 egg whites
1/2 cup superfine sugar
1/2 cup (2 oz.) hazelnuts, toasted, finely ground

Filling:
2 tablespoons unsalted butter, softened
3 tablespoons powdered sugar, sifted
1 egg yolk
1/4 cup (1 oz.) hazelnuts, toasted, finely ground

To Finish:
Sifted powdered sugar for sprinkling

Cut sheets of parchment or waxed paper to fit several baking sheets. Draw 2-inch circles on paper. Grease baking sheets; place paper, drawn-circles-side-down, on sheets. Preheat oven to 275F (135C). In a clean grease-free bowl, beat egg whites until very stiff, but not dry. Add 1/2 tablespoon of the sugar; beat until incorporated and meringue is stiff and shiny. Add remaining sugar, a little at a time, beating well after each addition.

Fold 1/2 cup hazelnuts into meringue. Spoon into piping bag fitted with a 3/8-inch-plain tip. Following drawn circles, pipe spirals of meringue onto prepared baking sheets. Bake 1-1/4 hours or until dry. Cool on baking sheets. To make filling, beat butter with powdered sugar in a small bowl until creamy. Beat in egg yolk and 1/4 cup hazelnuts. Remove meringues from paper; sandwich together with filling. Sprinkle lightly with powdered sugar.

Makes about 21 cookies.

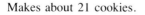

VALENTINE HEART

1/4 cup butter, softened
5 teaspoons sugar
2 egg yolks
1/2 teaspoon vanilla extract
3/4 cup all-purpose flour
2 tablespoons cornstarch
1/2 teaspoon baking powder

Icing:
2 egg whites
2-1/4 cups powdered sugar, sifted
Red food coloring

Decoration (non-edible):
1 deep pink rose
1 white rose
1 egg white, very lightly beaten
1/4 cup superfine sugar

To prepare decoration, gently remove petals from roses. Very lightly brush petals with beaten egg white; coat lightly with superfine sugar. Shake off excess sugar; place on waxed paper to dry.

Preheat oven to 350F (175C). Grease a large baking sheet with butter. In a medium-size bowl, beat butter with 5 teaspoons sugar until creamy. Beat in egg yolks and vanilla. Sift flour, cornstarch and baking powder into bowl; blend in with a spoon then mix with your hand to form a soft dough. Knead lightly on a floured surface until smooth. Roll out to an 11'' x 9'' rectangle. Place on prepared baking sheet.

Using a paper or cardboard template, cut out a large heart from dough. Remove trimmings. (Use to make small cookies, if desired.) Bake heart 20 minutes or until very lightly browned. Remove from baking sheet to a wire rack; cool.

When heart is cool, place rack over a baking sheet. To make icing, mix egg whites with 1 cup plus 2 tablespoons of the powdered sugar to make an icing thick enough to coat the back of a spoon evenly. Color icing a delicate pink with a few drops of red food coloring. Pour icing onto heart; spread out with a spatula to coat evenly. Leave on rack until icing sets. Spoon excess icing into a bowl; cover surface with plastic wrap. Set aside.

Just before icing is completely set, decorate heart with rose petals, pressing them gently into icing to secure. Beat remaining powdered sugar into excess icing. Spoon into a piping bag fitted with a small plain writing tip. Pipe your own valentine message on the heart. Pipe a decorative border around edge of heart.

Makes 1 Valentine Heart.

— TRADITIONAL SHORTBREAD —

1/2 cup butter, softened
5 teaspoons sugar
1-1/4 cups all-purpose flour
Pinch of salt
2 tablespoons fine semolina

To Finish:
Superfine sugar for sprinkling

In a medium-size bowl, beat butter with sugar until creamy. Sift flour and salt into bowl; add semolina. Blend in with a spoon then mix with your hand to form a soft dough.

Knead dough lightly on a floured surface until smooth. Roll out to a smooth circle, about 6 inches in diameter. Very lightly flour a 7-inch shortbread mold. Place shortbread smooth-side-down in mold. Press out to fit mold exactly. Very carefully unmold shortbread onto an ungreased baking sheet. Refrigerate 1 hour. If you do not have a shortbread mold, shape dough into a neat circle; place on baking sheet. Prick well with a fork then pinch edge to decorate.

Preheat oven to 325F (165C). Bake about 35 minutes or until cooked through. Shortbread should remain pale. As soon as shortbread is removed from oven, sprinkle very lightly with superfine sugar. Cool on baking sheet about 20 minutes then very carefully remove to a wire rack to cool completely.

Makes one (7-inch) shortbread.

— CHRISTMAS SHORTBREAD —

1-3/4 cups all-purpose flour
Pinch of salt
3 tablespoons cornstarch
1/4 cup sugar
1 cup butter

To Decorate:
34 blanched almonds
15 walnut halves
7 green candied cherries, cut in half
5 red candied cherries, cut in half

To Finish:
Superfine sugar for sprinkling

Sift flour, salt and cornstarch into a medium-size bowl; add sugar. Cut in butter until mixture forms coarse crumbs. Gently mix together to form a soft dough. Roll out dough on a floured surface to a circle slightly smaller than 10 inches in diameter. Place dough in a 10-inch-fluted pie pan with removable bottom. Press dough gently to fit pan exactly, pressing well into flutes. Smooth with the back of a spoon. Prick well with a fork.

To decorate shortbread, arrange almonds in a neat ring around edge of dough. Add a ring of walnut halves, a ring of green cherries, then a ring of red cherries. Place a walnut half in the center. Refrigerate shortbread 30 minutes. Preheat oven to 350F (175C). Bake shortbread about 45 minutes or until lightly browned. Cool in pan. Sprinkle lightly with superfine sugar. Carefully remove from pan onto a serving plate.

Makes about 16 servings.

— CHRISTMAS TREE COOKIES —

2/3 cup butter, softened
1/3 cup sugar
3 egg yolks
2 teaspoons orange flower water
2 cups all-purpose flour
1 teaspoon baking powder

Decoration:
2 egg whites
3 cups powdered sugar, sifted
Edible gold and white glitter
Thin ribbon, various colors

Preheat oven to 350F (175C). Grease several baking sheets with butter.

In a medium-size bowl, beat butter with 1/3 cup sugar until creamy. Beat in egg yolks and orange flower water. Sift flour and baking powder into bowl; blend in with a spoon then mix with your hand to form a soft dough. Knead lightly on a floured surface until smooth. Roll out to 1/8-inch thickness. Using 2-1/2-inch-shaped cookie cutters, cut out shapes such as circles, stars and hearts from dough. Place on prepared baking sheets. Knead and roll out trimmings; cut out more shapes. Continue until dough is used up.

Using a skewer or plastic straw, make a small hole about 1/2 inch from the top edge of each shape. Be sure hole is large enough to thread ribbon through. Bake cookies 15 to 18 minutes or until very lightly browned. Remove from baking sheets to wire racks; cool.

To decorate cookies, mix egg whites with 2 cups of the powdered sugar in a medium-size bowl. Icing should be thick enough to coat the back of a spoon. Brush icing thinly and evenly over each cookie. Let icing set. Meanwhile, beat remaining powdered sugar into remaining icing, beating until icing forms stiff peaks. Cover with plastic wrap to prevent drying.

On two small saucers, blend gold and white glitter with water to make a smooth thin paste. Paint cookies with glitters. Allow to dry.

Decorate shapes with reserved icing by adding it in small flecks or by piping it on; let icing set. Thread cookies onto colored ribbons and hang on the Christmas tree. If cookies are left on the tree too long they will dry out. So keep a supply of fresh cookies in an airtight container to replenish the tree.

Makes about 28 Christmas Tree Cookies.

EASTER COOKIES

3/4 cup butter, softened
3/4 cup sugar
3 egg yolks
4 teaspoons orange flower water
2 tablespoons milk
3/4 cup (4 oz.) currants
4 cups all-purpose flour
Pinch of salt

Glaze:
1 egg white, very lightly beaten
2 tablespoons superfine sugar

Preheat oven to 350F (175C). Grease several baking sheets with butter. In a large bowl, beat butter with sugar until creamy. Beat in egg yolks, orange flower water and milk.

Add currants. Sift flour and salt into bowl; mix in to form a fairly stiff dough. Knead lightly on a floured surface until smooth. Roll out to 1/8-inch thickness. Using a round 2-1/2-inch-fluted cookie cutter, cut out circles from dough; place on prepared baking sheets. Knead and roll out trimmings; cut out more circles. Continue until dough is used up.

Bake cookies 10 minutes. Remove from oven. Brush cookies with beaten egg white; sprinkle lightly with superfine sugar. Return to oven for about 5 minutes longer or until lightly browned. Remove from baking sheets to wire racks; cool. Store in an airtight container.

Makes about 54 cookies.

EASTER BUNNIES

1/2 cup butter, softened
1/2 cup sugar
1 egg, beaten
1 teaspoon vanilla extract
2/3 cup finely shredded coconut
2 cups all-purpose flour
Pinch of salt
1/2 teaspoon baking powder

To Finish:
Sifted powdered sugar for sprinkling

Preheat oven to 350F (175C). Grease several baking sheets with butter. In a large bowl, beat butter with sugar until creamy. Beat in egg and vanilla.

Stir in coconut. Sift flour, salt and baking powder into creamed mixture. Blend in with a spoon then mix with your hand to form a soft dough. Knead lightly on a floured surface until smooth. Roll out dough to 1/8-inch thickness. Using a rabbit-shaped cookie cutter, cut out rabbits from dough; place on prepared baking sheets. Knead and roll out trimmings; cut out more rabbits. Continue until dough is used up.

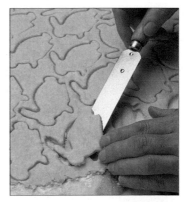

Bake 15 minutes or until very lightly browned. Remove from baking sheets to wire racks; cool. When cool, sprinkle lightly with powdered sugar, if desired.

Makes up to 60 cookies, depending on size of cookie cutter used.

ADVENT CRESCENTS

2 cups all-purpose flour
Pinch of salt
1/2 cup sugar
1-1/3 cups (5 oz.) ground almonds
1 cup butter, cut in small cubes
3 egg yolks
A few drops almond extract

To Finish:
Sifted powdered sugar for sprinkling

Sift flour and salt into a large bowl; mix in sugar and ground almonds. Make a well in the center.

Add butter, egg yolks and almond extract to the well. Using your fingertips, gently mix butter with egg yolks, gradually incorporating flour mixture until a soft dough forms. Wrap dough in plastic wrap; refrigerate 30 minutes. Preheat oven to 350F (175C).

Shape dough into walnut-size balls, then into thin rolls each about 4 inches long. Curve rolls into a crescent shape. Place on ungreased baking sheets. Bake crescents 15 minutes or until lightly browned. Cool on baking sheets. Sprinkle heavily with powdered sugar. Remove from baking sheets to a serving plate.

Makes about 42 crescents.

——— LEBKUCHEN HEART ———

3 cups self-rising flour
2 teaspoons ground allspice
Pinch of salt
1/4 cup clear honey
1 cup packed dark brown sugar
3 tablespoons butter
1 egg, beaten
Finely grated peel of 1 lemon
1 tablespoon lemon juice

To Decorate:
8 oz. semisweet chocolate, melted
1 egg white
1-1/2 cups powdered sugar, sifted
Silver dragées

Preheat oven to 350F (175C). Grease a large baking sheet with butter. Sift flour, allspice and salt into a large bowl; make a well in the center. Put honey, brown sugar and butter in a small saucepan; stir over low heat until melted. Cool slightly. Pour into well; add beaten egg, lemon peel and juice. Mix to form a soft dough. Knead on a floured surface until smooth. Roll out dough to an 11" x 9" rectangle. Place on prepared baking sheet. Using a paper or cardboard template, cut out a large heart shape.

Remove trimmings from around heart; use to make Gingerbread Men (page 49). Bake heart 20 to 25 minutes or until lightly browned. Remove to wire rack; cool. When cool, place rack over a large baking sheet; coat heart with melted chocolate. Allow chocolate to set. In a medium-size bowl, beat egg white with powdered sugar until mixture forms stiff peaks. Decorate heart, simply or elaborately, with icing and silver dragées.

Makes 1 Lebkuchen Heart.

─── GINGERBREAD HOUSE ───

2 recipes Lebkuchen Heart dough (page 93)
Cardboard templates for Gingerbread House,
   as shown on page 97

Royal Icing:
4 egg whites
6 cups (2 lbs.) powdered sugar, sifted
2 teaspoons lemon juice
2 teaspoons glycerine

Decorations:
20 long thin crisp mint-flavored chocolate sticks
Assorted fruit candies
22 walnut halves
14 blanched almonds
Round candy-coated chocolate pieces
2 small chocolate flake bars

Preheat oven to 350F (175C). Grease three (13''
x 9'') baking pans with butter. If you only have
one pan, bake one pan of dough at a time.
Divide dough into 3 equal-size pieces. Roll out
each one on a well-floured surface to a rectangle
slightly smaller than 13'' x 9''. Trim edges to
make straight; place each dough in its pan. Bake
about 20 minutes or until lightly browned. To be
able to cut baked dough in shapes without hurry-
ing, stagger baking times by placing pans in
oven at 10 minute intervals.

While dough is still warm, cut dough in first pan into shapes as shown in Figure 1. Cut dough in second pan into shapes as shown in Figure 2. Cut dough in third pan into shapes as shown in Figure 3. Cool shapes in pans. When cutting out Christmas trees, cut 1 in half lengthwise.

To make icing, lightly beat egg whites in a medium-size bowl. Gradually beat in powdered sugar, lemon juice and glycerine to make a stiff icing. Cover bowl with a clean damp towel to prevent drying. Using icing to secure pieces, assemble house as follows. Secure corner supports to inside of the front panel and back panel.

Secure side panels to outer edges of corner supports. Place on a 12-inch-square cake board.

Spread a little icing over one side panel. Cut mint sticks to fit top and bottom of windows. Decorate with fruit candies and walnuts as desired. Repeat on second side.

Decorate front panel in a similar way, decorating corners with almonds. Decorate end panel. Fix roof panels in position.

Stick chimney pieces together; fix in position on roof. Cover roof with icing. Decorate with candy-coated chocolate pieces and fruit candies.

Stick cut Christmas tree halves to each side of the whole tree; cover with icing. Spread icing on the cake board outside of house. Fix tree in position.

Cut chocolate flakes to represent logs. Place in position on cake board. Leave house overnight to dry.

Makes 1 Gingerbread House.

Figure 1

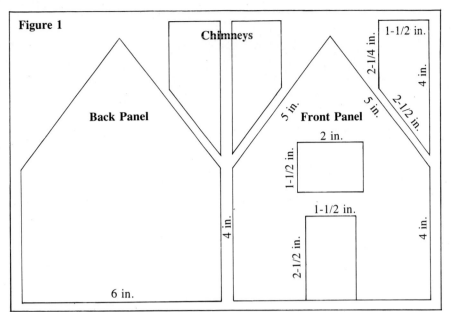

Chimneys

Back Panel

Front Panel

1-1/2 in.

2-1/4 in.

4 in.

5 in.

5 in.

2-1/2 in.

2 in.

1-1/2 in.

4 in.

1-1/2 in.

2-1/2 in.

4 in.

4 in.

6 in.

13 in.

Figure 2

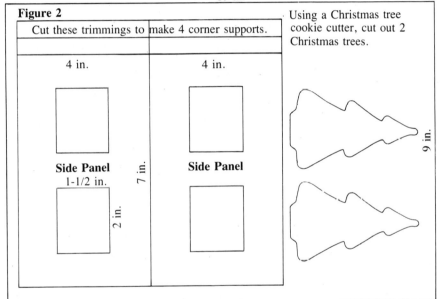

Cut these trimmings to make 4 corner supports.

Using a Christmas tree cookie cutter, cut out 2 Christmas trees.

4 in.

4 in.

Side Panel

1-1/2 in.

Side Panel

7 in.

2 in.

9 in.

Figure 3

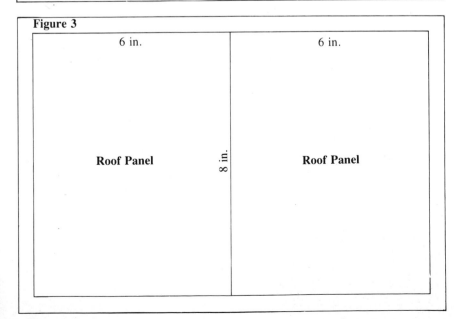

6 in.

6 in.

Roof Panel

8 in.

Roof Panel

SPICED OAT COOKIES

3/4 cup butter, softened
1 cup packed dark brown sugar
1 teaspoon vanilla extract
1 egg
1/2 cup self-rising flour
Pinch of salt
1/2 teaspoon baking soda
1 tablespoon ground cinnamon
2-3/4 cups rolled oats

To Finish:
Sifted powdered sugar for sprinkling

Preheat oven to 350F (175C). Grease several baking sheets with butter. In a large bowl, beat butter with brown sugar until creamy. Beat in vanilla and egg. Sift flour, salt, baking soda and cinnamon into bowl; blend in with a spoon.

Add rolled oats: mix with your hand to form a soft dough. If dough is too soft to roll out, chill until firm. Roll out dough on a floured surface to 1/4-inch thickness. Using a 2-inch-round cookie cutter, cut out circles from dough; place on prepared baking sheets. Knead and roll out trimmings; cut out more circles. Continue until dough is used up.

Bake cookies about 25 minutes or until lightly browned. Cool on baking sheets a few minutes then remove to wire racks to cool completely. Sprinkle powdered sugar lightly over cookies.

Makes about 35 cookies.

MUESLI COOKIES

3/4 cup butter, softened
1/3 cup sugar
1/4 cup clear honey
Finely grated peel of 1 medium-size orange
1 egg
1/2 cup self-rising flour
Pinch of salt
3 cups muesli

Preheat oven to 350F (175C). Grease several baking sheets with butter. In a large bowl, beat butter with sugar until creamy. Beat in honey, orange peel and egg. Sift flour and salt into bowl; blend in with a spoon.

Add muesli to creamed mixture. Mix with your hand to form a soft dough. Roll out dough on a floured surface to 1/4-inch thickness. Using a 2-1/2-inch-round cookie cutter, cut out circles from dough; place on prepared baking sheets. Knead and roll out trimmings; cut out more circles. Continue until dough is used up.

Bake about 20 minutes or until very lightly browned. Cool on baking sheets a few minutes then remove to wire racks to cool completely.

Makes about 30 cookies.

HONEY DOUBLES

1/2 cup self-rising flour
1 teaspoon baking soda
1/3 cup packed dark brown sugar
2 cups rolled oats
1/3 cup butter
1/4 cup plus 2 teaspoons clear honey, heated
   then cooled
1 teaspoon vanilla extract

Filling:
1/4 cup unsalted butter, softened
1/2 cup powdered sugar, sifted
1 tablespoon clear honey
2 teaspoons lemon juice

Preheat oven to 350F (175C). Grease several
baking sheets with butter. Sift flour, baking
soda and brown sugar into a large bowl. Mix in
rolled oats. Cut in butter until mixture resembles
coarse bread crumbs. Add honey and vanilla;
mix to form a soft dough. Roll out dough on a
floured surface to 1/8-inch thickness. Using a
2-inch-round cookie cutter, cut out circles from
dough; place on prepared baking sheets. Knead
and roll out trimmings; cut out more circles.
Continue until dough is used up. Bake 8 to 12
minutes or until lightly browned. Remove to
wire racks; cool.

To make filling, beat butter with powdered
sugar in a small bowl until creamy. Beat in
honey and lemon juice. Refrigerate about 20
minutes to make a stiff filling. Sandwich cookies together with honey filling. Keep cookies
cool to prevent filling from softening.

Makes about 16 cookies.

——— BRAN COOKIES ———

2 cups bran cereal
1/3 cup packed brown sugar
1 cup self-rising flour
1/3 cup butter, softened
1/3 cup currants
1 egg, beaten
Milk for brushing

To Finish:
Superfine sugar for sprinkling

Preheat oven to 350F (175C). Grease several baking sheets with butter. Put bran cereal in a food processor or blender and process until fine.

Add sugar and flour; process a few seconds longer to blend ingredients. Add butter; process until mixture resembles coarse bread crumbs. Add currants and egg; process until mixture forms a soft dough. Roll out dough on a floured surface to 1/8-inch thickness. Using a round 2-1/2-inch-fluted cookie cutter, cut out circles from dough; place on prepared baking sheets. Knead and roll out trimmings; cut out more circles. Continue until dough is used up.

Brush each cookie with a little milk to glaze. Bake about 20 minutes or until lightly browned. As soon as cookies are removed from oven, sprinkle with superfine sugar. Cool on baking sheets a few minutes then remove to wire racks to cool completely.

Makes about 32 cookies.

—— PEANUT & RAISIN BARS ——

3/4 cup butter
1/4 cup packed brown sugar
1/3 cup clear honey
3/4 cup mixed peanuts and raisins, roughly
** chopped**
2-3/4 cups rolled oats

Preheat oven to 400F (205C). Grease a 13'' x 9'' baking pan with butter. Put butter, sugar and honey in a large saucepan; stir over a low heat until butter melts and sugar dissolves. Stir in peanuts and raisins.

Stir in rolled oats. Spread mixture evenly in prepared pan. Bake 20 minutes or until golden brown. Using a sharp knife, mark surface of mixture with lines to use as a guide for cutting. Leave mixture in pan until completely cool.

To remove from pan, cut through marked lines; remove bars with a small flexible spatula. Instead of using peanuts and raisins, other nuts such as walnuts, almonds, or hazelnuts may be substituted for the peanuts. Alternatively, use all nuts or all raisins.

Makes 30 bars.

RAISIN COOKIES

1-1/3 cups whole-wheat flour
1/2 cup rolled oats, finely ground
1/4 cup demerara (brown) sugar
Pinch of salt
1 teaspoon baking powder
1/2 cup butter, softened
1/3 cup raisins
1 egg, beaten

Preheat oven to 375F (190C). Grease several baking sheets with butter. Put flour, oatmeal, sugar, salt and baking powder in a medium-size bowl; mix well.

Cut butter into flour until mixture resembles fine bread crumbs. Mix in raisins. Add egg; mix to form a soft dough. Roll out dough on a floured surface to 1/8-inch thickness. Using a 2-1/2-inch-round cookie cutter, cut out circles from dough; place on prepared baking sheets. Knead and roll out trimmings; cut out more circles. Continue until dough is used up.

Bake about 15 minutes or until lightly browned. Cool on baking sheets a few minutes then remove to wire racks to cool completely. If preferred, raisins may be omitted.

Makes about 22 cookies.

—— SESAME SEED CRACKERS ——

1-3/4 cups whole-wheat flour
1/2 teaspoon salt
1/2 teaspoon baking powder
1/3 cup butter, softened
1 egg, beaten
2 tablespoons milk, plus a little extra for
    brushing
1/4 cup (1 oz.) sesame seeds

Preheat oven to 350F (175C). Grease several baking sheets with butter. Mix flour, salt and baking powder together in a medium-size bowl.

Cut butter into flour until mixture resembles fine bread crumbs. Add egg and 2 tablespoons milk; mix to form a stiff dough. Roll out dough on a floured surface to 1/8-inch thickness. Using a 2-1/2-inch-round cookie cutter, cut out circles from dough; place on prepared baking sheets. Knead and roll out trimmings; cut out more circles. Continue until dough is used up.

Brush crackers with a little milk, then sprinkle evenly with sesame seed. Bake about 15 minutes or until lightly browned. Remove to wire racks; cool. Serve with cheese or pâté.

Makes about 20 cookies.

SCOTTISH OATCAKES

1 cup rolled oats
1/2 teaspoon baking powder
Pinch of salt
2 tablespoons butter, softened
2 tablespoons boiling water

Put rolled oats, baking powder and salt in a medium-size bowl: cut in butter until mixture resembles coarse bread crumbs. Add boiling water; mix to form a sticky dough. Knead until oats absorb water and dough becomes drier and smoother.

Roll out dough on a lightly floured surface to a circle about 8 inches in diameter. Using a plate as a guide, cut dough in a neat circle. Cut circle in 8 equal-size pieces, forming neat triangles.

Heat a griddle over medium heat; grease very lightly. Place oatcakes on griddle. Cook 8 to 10 minutes or until cooked through and corners curl up. Cool on a wire rack. Serve with butter and jam.

Makes 8 Scottish Oatcakes

CHEESE STRAWS

1 cup all-purpose flour
1/2 teaspoon baking powder
Pinch of salt
Pinch of cayenne pepper
1/4 teaspoon dry mustard
3/4 cup (3-1/2 oz.) grated Parmesan cheese
1/3 cup butter, softened
3 egg yolks
2 teaspoons water
1 egg white, very lightly beaten

To Finish:
Paprika for sprinkling

Preheat oven to 400F (205C). Grease several baking sheets with butter.

Sift flour, baking powder, salt, cayenne and dry mustard into a bowl; mix in all but 1 tablespoon of Parmesan cheese. Cut in butter until mixture resembles fine bread crumbs. Add egg yolks and water; mix to form a dough. Roll out dough on a floured surface to a 13'' x 9'' rectangle. Trim edges to make straight. Brush with egg white and sprinkle with remaining Parmesan cheese. To make straws, cut in half lengthwise. To make twists, cut in half crosswise.

For straws: cut across each piece into 1/4-inch strips. For twists: cut in long thin strips then twist together in twos. Place on prepared baking sheets. Knead and roll out trimmings. To make rings, use 2-1/2-inch-round and 1-3/4-inch-round cookie cutters; cut out 10 rings. Place on prepared baking sheets. Bake 8 to 10 minutes or until just lightly browned. Remove to wire racks; cool. Sprinkle lightly with paprika. Fill rings with straws.

Makes about 100 straws.

ANCHOVY & RED PEPPER
TWISTS

1 red bell pepper
1 cup all-purpose flour
Pinch of salt
Pinch of cayenne pepper
1/4 teaspoon dry mustard
1/2 cup (2 oz.) shredded Cheddar cheese
1/3 cup butter, softened
3 egg yolks
2 teaspoons water
3 (2-oz.) cans anchovy fillets, well-drained
1 egg white, very lightly beaten

Cook whole red bell pepper under a hot broiler, turning frequently, until skin wrinkles and scorches slightly. Cool. Remove skin and seeds. Cut flesh in thin strips about 1/4 inch wide and 4 inches long.

Sift flour, salt, cayenne and dry mustard into a medium-size bowl; mix in cheese. Cut in butter until mixture resembles fine bread crumbs. Add egg yolks and water; mix to form a dough. Roll out dough on a floured surface to a 13'' x 9'' rectangle. Trim edges to make straight. Cut in half lengthwise. Cutting across strips, cut in thin strips, about 1/4 inch wide.

Preheat oven to 400F (205C). Grease several baking sheets with butter. Cut anchovy fillets in half lengthwise. Take a pastry strip and a strip of bell pepper and very carefully twist together. Place on prepared baking sheet. Repeat with remaining bell pepper strips and anchovies. Brush twists with beaten egg white. Bake about 10 minutes or until golden brown. Remove from baking sheets to wire racks; cool. These twists should be eaten the same day they are baked.

Makes about 70 twists.

WATER CRACKERS

1-1/2 cups all-purpose flour
1/2 teaspoon salt
1 teaspoon baking powder
3 tablespoons butter, softened
4 tablespoons water

Preheat oven to 350F (175C). Grease several baking sheets with butter. Sift flour, salt and baking powder into a medium-size bowl; cut in butter until mixture resembles fine bread crumbs. Add water; mix to form a dough.

Knead dough on a floured surface until smooth. Roll out very thinly. Prick well with a fork. Using a round 3-1/2-inch cookie cutter, cut out circles from dough; place on prepared baking sheets. Knead and roll out trimmings; cut out more circles. Continue until dough is used up.

Bake about 15 minutes or until well cooked and only slightly browned. Remove to wire racks; cool. Serve with cheese or pâté.

Makes about 20 cookies.

CANAPÉ OATCAKES

1/2 cup all-purpose flour
1 teaspoon baking powder
Pinch of salt
1 cup rolled oats, finely ground
1/4 cup butter
2 tablespoons boiling water

Preheat oven to 350F (175C). Grease several baking sheets with butter. Sift flour, baking powder and salt into a medium-size bowl; mix in rolled oats . Cut in butter until mixture resembles coarse bread crumbs. Add water; mix to form a dough. Knead until oats absorb water and dough becomes drier and smoother.

Roll out dough on a lightly floured surface to 1/8-inch thickness. Using a round 1-3/4-inch cookie cutter, cut out small circles from dough; place on prepared baking sheets. Knead and roll out trimmings; cut out more circles. Continue until dough is used up. Bake about 15 minutes or until cooked through. Remove from baking sheets to wire racks; cool.

To serve, spread canapés with plain or flavored butter. Top with savory fillings, such as small pieces of smoked salmon, cream cheese, caviar, pâté, small rolls of ham or other smoked meats, or sliced hard-cooked eggs. Garnish with lettuce, cucumber, onions, tomato, parsley, etc. The combinations are simply endless.

Makes about 36 canapés.

———— BLUE-CHEESE NIBBLES ————

1 cup all-purpose flour
1/4 teaspoon salt
A small pinch of cayenne pepper
1/2 teaspoon baking powder
1/3 cup butter, softened
3 oz. blue cheese, crumbled
3 egg yolks
2 teaspoons water
1 teaspoon mixed Italian seasoning

To Finish:
Salt for sprinkling
Celery salt for sprinkling

Preheat oven to 400F (205C). Grease several baking sheets with butter.

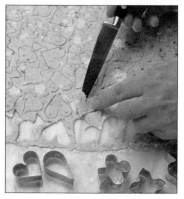

Sift flour, salt, cayenne and baking powder into a medium-size bowl. Cut in butter and cheese until mixture resembles coarse crumbs. Add egg yolks and water; mix to form a dough. Divide dough in half; knead Italian seasoning into one half. Knead doughs lightly on a floured surface until smooth. Roll out thinly. Cut in small shapes using aspic cutters, or cut with a knife in small squares, triangles or diamond shapes. Place on prepared baking sheets. Knead and roll out trimmings; cut out more shapes. Continue until dough is used up

Bake 8 to 10 minutes or until lightly browned. As soon as nibbles are removed from oven, sprinkle salt over the herb nibbles; sprinkle celery salt over the plain ones. Cool on baking sheets. Serve with before-dinner drinks.

Makes about 120 nibbles depending on size of cutter.

SESAME STICKS

1-1/2 cups all-purpose flour
1/2 teaspoon baking powder
1/2 teaspoon salt
1/3 cup butter, softened
4 tablespoons boiling water
1 small egg, beaten
1/2 cup sesame seed

Preheat oven to 350F (175C). Grease several baking sheets with butter. Sift flour, baking powder and salt into a medium-size bowl. Cut in butter until mixture resembles fine bread crumbs. Add boiling water; mix to form a soft dough.

Knead dough lightly on a floured surface until smooth. Divide into 18 equal-size pieces. Roll each piece of dough into a long thin strand, about 12 to 14 inches long; place on prepared baking sheets. Brush strands with beaten egg.

Sprinkle evenly with sesame seed. Bake 20 minutes or until lightly browned. Remove carefully to wire racks; cool. Serve with before-dinner drinks.

Makes 18 Sesame Sticks.

CARAWAY PRETZELS

1-1/2 cups all-purpose flour
1/2 teaspoon baking powder
1/2 teaspoon salt
1/3 cup butter, softened
1 tablespoon caraway seeds
4 tablespoons boiling water
1 egg white, very lightly beaten

Preheat oven to 350F (175C). Grease several baking sheets with butter. Sift flour, baking powder and salt into a medium-size bowl. Cut in butter until mixture resembles fine bread crumbs; mix in 1 teaspoon of the caraway seeds. Add boiling water; mix to form a soft dough.

Knead dough lightly on a floured surface until smooth. Divide into 36 equal-size pieces. Take 1 piece of dough, shape into a long thin strand about 8 inches long. Bring ends around to form a loop; cross over then take back up to top of loop. Press ends firmly into position to secure. Place on prepared baking sheet. Repeat with remaining pieces of dough.

Brush pretzels with egg white; sprinkle evenly with remaining caraway seeds. Bake 18 to 20 minutes or until lightly browned. Carefully remove from baking sheets to wire racks; cool.

Makes about 36 pretzels.

— ONION & GARLIC TWISTS —

1/3 cup butter, softened
2 garlic cloves, crushed
2 teaspoons very finely grated onion
3 egg yolks
2 teaspoons water
1-1/2 cups all-purpose flour
1/2 teaspoon baking powder
1/4 teaspoon salt
1 egg white, very lightly beaten
Coarse salt for sprinkling

Preheat oven to 400F (205C). Grease several baking sheets with butter. In a medium-size bowl, beat butter until creamy.

Beat in garlic, onion, egg yolks and water. Sift flour, baking powder and salt into bowl; blend in with a spoon then mix with your hand to form a soft dough. Knead lightly on a floured surface until smooth. Roll out to a 14'' x 10'' rectangle. Trim edges to make straight. Cut in half crosswise. Using a pastry wheel or a knife, cut dough in thin strips, about 7'' x 1/4''.

One strip at a time, carefully twist strips; place on prepared baking sheets. Brush with beaten egg white and sprinkle lightly with coarse salt. Bake 15 minutes or until lightly browned. Very carefully remove from baking sheets to wire racks; cool.

Makes 30 to 36 twists.

— CHEESE & HERB COOKIES —

1 cup all-purpose flour
1/2 teaspoon baking powder
1/4 teaspoon salt
1/3 cup butter, softened
3/4 cup (3 oz.) shredded Cheddar cheese
3 egg yolks
2 teaspoons water

Filling:
3 tablespoons butter, softened
1 teaspoon fresh snipped chives
1/2 teaspoon mixed Italian seasoning
1/3 cup (1-1/2 oz.) shredded Cheddar cheese

To Finish:
Paprika for sprinkling

Preheat oven to 400F (205C). Grease several baking sheets with butter. Sift flour, baking powder and salt into a medium-size bowl. Cut in butter until mixture resembles fine bread crumbs; mix in cheese. Add egg yolks and water; mix to form a dough. Knead lightly on a floured surface until smooth. Roll out thinly. Prick well with a fork. Using a round 2-inch cookie cutter, cut out circles from dough; place on prepared baking sheets. Knead and roll out trimmings; cut out more circles. Continue until dough is used up.

Bake about 10 minutes or until lightly browned. Remove cookies to wire racks; cool. To make filling, beat butter, chives and Italian seasoning in a small bowl until creamy. Beat in cheese. Season well with salt and pepper. Sandwich cookies together with filling. Sprinkle lightly with paprika. Keep cool.

Makes about 30 cookies.

CURRY COOKIES

1-1/2 cups all-purpose flour
1/2 teaspoon baking powder
1/4 teaspoon salt
2 teaspoons curry powder
1/3 cup butter, softened
1 egg
1 teaspoon tomato paste

Preheat oven to 400F (205C). Grease several baking sheets with butter. Sift flour, baking powder, salt and curry powder into a medium-size bowl. Cut in butter until mixture resembles fine bread crumbs. Make a well in the center.

In a small bowl, beat egg and tomato paste together. Pour into well. Mix to make a soft dough. Knead lightly on a floured surface until smooth. Roll out to 1/8-inch thickness. Using a pastry wheel or a sharp knife, cut dough in 3'' x 1-3/4'' rectangles; place on prepared sheets. Knead and roll out trimmings; cut out more rectangles. Continue until dough is used up.

Bake cookies 12 to 15 minutes or until very lightly browned. Remove from baking sheets to wire racks; cool. Serve with cheese or savory dips.

Makes about 30 cookies.

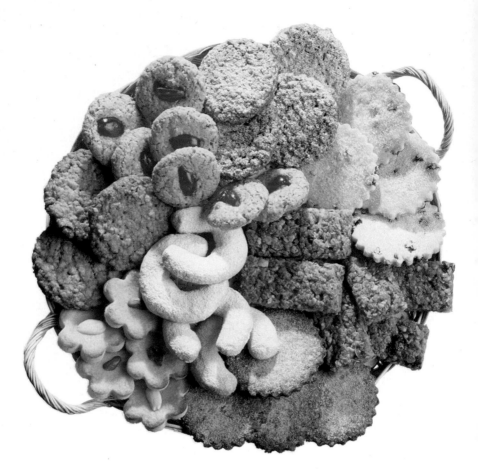

Clockwise from top: Spiced Oat Cookies, page 98; Easter Cookies, page 90; Peanut & Raisin Bar, Page 102; Bran Cookies, page 101; Advent Crescents, page 92; Almond Flowers, page 46; Muesli Cookies, page 99; Hazelnut Cookies, page 78.

Clockwise from top: Vanilla Sticks, page 59; Triple Orange Drops, page 60; Shrewsbury Cookies, page 41; Viennese Fingers, page 56; Chocolate Pretzels, page 48; Pinwheels, page 47; Cherry Praline Rings, page 40.

Clockwise from top: Pistachio Rings, page 76; Chocolate Dreams, page 68; Café Sternen, page 79; Walnut-Chocolate Cookies, page 77; Orange & Chocolate Rings, page 66; Flavored Spritz Cookies, page 64.

Clockwise from top: Cheese Straws, page 106; Curry Cookies, page 115; Sesame
Seed Crackers, page 104; Water Crackers, page 108.

INDEX